experience and a passion for travel.

**Rely on Thomas Cook as your travelling companion on your next trip and benefit from our unique heritage.**

Thomas Cook **pocket** guides

# GRAN CANARIA

Your travelling companion since 1873

Thomas Cook

**Written by Brian and Eileen Anderson, updated by Joe Cawley**

**Published by Thomas Cook Publishing**
A division of Thomas Cook Tour Operations Limited
Company registration no. 3772199 England
The Thomas Cook Business Park, Unit 9, Coningsby Road,
Peterborough PE3 8SB, United Kingdom
Email: books@thomascook.com, Tel: +44 (0) 1733 416477
www.thomascookpublishing.com

**Produced by Cambridge Publishing Management Limited**
Burr Elm Court, Main Street, Caldecote CB23 7NU
www.cambridgepm.co.uk

ISBN: 978-1-84848-399-6



Series Editor: Karen Beaulah
Production/DTP: Steven Collins

Printed and bound in Spain by GraphyCems

Cover photography © Travel Library Limited/SuperStock

# CONTENTS

## WHAT'S IN YOUR GUIDEBOOK?

**Independent authors** Impartial, up-to-date information from our travel experts who meticulously source local knowledge.

**Experience** Thomas Cook's 165 years in the travel industry and guidebook publishing enriches every word with expertise you can trust.

**Travel know-how** Thomas Cook has thousands of staff working around the globe, all living and breathing travel.

**Editors** Travel-publishing professionals, pulling everything together to craft a perfect blend of words, pictures, maps and design.

**You, the traveller** We deliver a practical, no-nonsense approach to information, geared to how you really use it.

*One of Gran Canaria's traditional windmills*

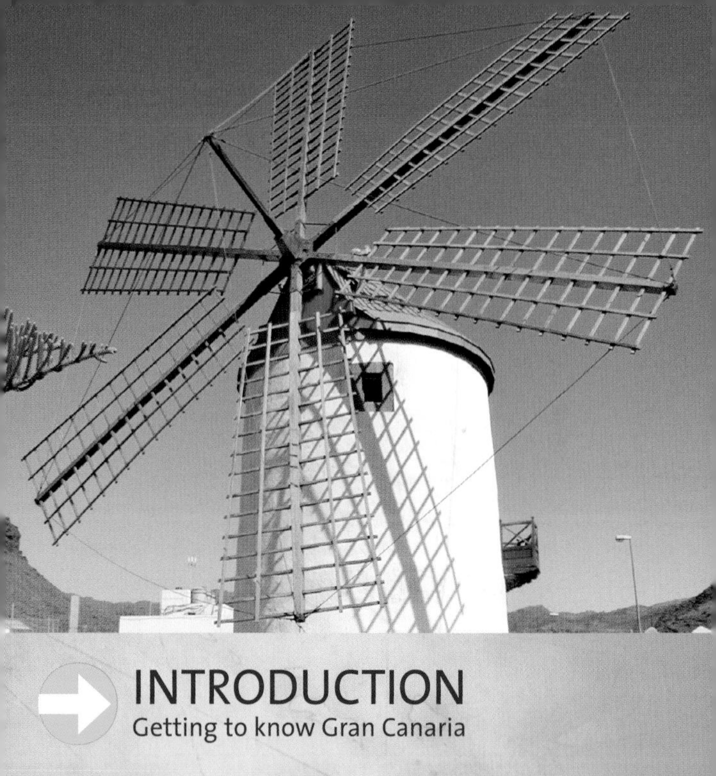

# INTRODUCTION
## Getting to know Gran Canaria

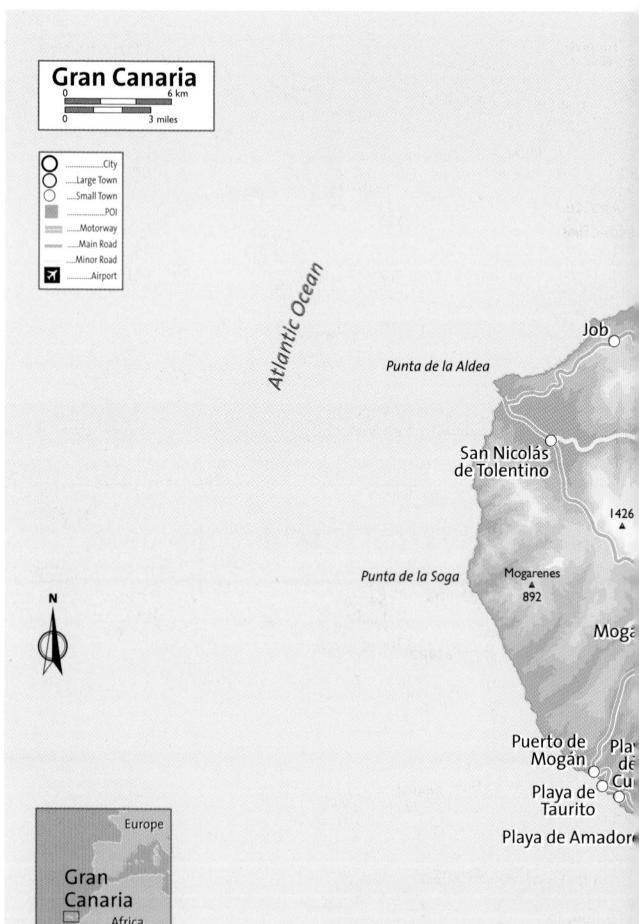
Gran Canaria
0
6 km
0
3 miles
City
Large Town
Small Town
POI
Motorway
Main Road
Minor Road
Airport
Atlantic Ocean
Job
Punta de la Aldea
San Nicolás de Tolentino
1426
Punta de la Soga
Mogarenes
892
N
Puerto de Mogán
Playa de Taurito
Playa de Amador
Europe
Gran Canaria
Africa

Punta de Gáldar
Punta de Guanarteme
Punta de la Vieja
Punta del Camello
Gáldar
Sardina
Santa María de Guía
Tinoca
LAS PALMAS
Cueva Pintada
Cenobio de Valerón
uerto de s Nieves
Arucas
Agaete
Firgas
Tamaraceite
edo de Dios
Monte Coello
GC1
Teror
Jardín Botánico Canario
Tafira Baja
Valleseco
Tafira Alta
Santa Brígida
Artenara
1771
Caldera Bandama
La Atalaya
Cruz de Tejeda
Telde
Vega de San Mateo
Tejeda
Roque Bentaiga
Roque Nublo
1949
Pozo de las Nieves
GC1
Cuatro Puertas
Ayacata
Gran Canaria Airport
Barranco de Guayadeque
Presa de Soria
Ingenio
Punta de Gando
San Bartolomé de Tirajana
Santa Lucía
Agüimes
Museo de Piedra y Artesanía
Fataga
Parque de Cocodrilos
Necrópolis de Arteara
Fataga Valley
Forteleza de Ansite
Arinaga
Arteara
Sardina
Vecindario
Palmitos Park
Mundo Aborigen
Sioux City
GC1
Punta de Tenefe
quapark uerto Rico
Aqualand
Bahía Feliz
Gran Karting
GC1
Playa del Inglés
San Agustín
rguineguin
Maspalomas
Meloneras

# Getting to know Gran Canaria

The Canaries are divided into eastern and western provinces, with Gran Canaria in the east (along with Lanzarote and Fuerteventura) and Tenerife in the west (with the smaller islands of La Gomera, El Hierro and La Palma). The islands of the eastern province have a hot, dry African climate, which makes them different in character from the wetter and greener islands of the western province. The massive dune systems at Maspalomas, on Gran Canaria, are a continuation of the Sahara Desert, yet this island's high volcanic peaks can also be covered in snow in the winter.

Gran Canaria is the third largest of the Canary Islands, at 1,560 sq km (602 sq miles), sharing the status of joint capital of the Canaries with neighbouring Tenerife. However, it has the largest population, with around 800,000 people.

Gran Canaria's year-round warmth and vast beaches of golden sand bring holidaymakers from all over Europe who want to build up a suntan. It also attracts people who want to escape from the crowded beaches and enjoy a measure of solitude. The island is excellent for walking, with spectacular volcanic landscapes to explore in the mountainous interior, as well as wild and undeveloped beaches in the north.

### THE SPORTING LIFE

Gran Canaria is perfect for watersports. Gently shelving beaches in the south are ideal for swimmers and novice windsurfers. In the north, Atlantic swells break against buried reefs to create waves mighty enough to attract keen surfers. There are also opportunities for sailing and deep-sea fishing. Sports enthusiasts are catered for, with chances to play golf, enjoy some fine walking, go horse riding or even ride a camel!

### SHOPPERS' PARADISE

For those in search of retail therapy, this island is the nearest thing to heaven. There are plenty of shopping centres, and the island is a vast, duty-free emporium with bargains to be had almost everywhere.

## LUNAR LANDSCAPES

On the drive from airport to resort, visitors often comment on the peculiar landscape, likening it to the moon. The hot, dry lower slopes are particularly barren and it is hard to believe that the interior hides spectacular landscapes – but it certainly does!

The island is roughly circular in shape and the whole of the central region is mountainous. The highest peak reaches an altitude of almost 1,950 m (6,394 ft). Deep ravines, or *barrancos*, rise high into the mountains and drop down in breathtaking descent towards the sea all around the island.

## THE PERFECT CLIMATE

Trade winds blowing from the northeast control the island's climate for most of the year. The mountains trap most of the moisture out of the winds as cloud, leaving the south to enjoy the very best of the island's sunshine. Sheltered areas in the south claim to have as many as 350 sunny days per year.

The island's climate is gentle throughout all seasons, with summer temperatures around 23–25°C (73–77°F) and winter just two or three degrees cooler. The near-constant trade winds temper the heat. Puerto Rico, in the southwest, is often sheltered from breezes and is a good place to go on days when the breeze is too strong elsewhere.

## FLORA

The flora on the island is unique and very different from that seen in the Mediterranean. Palm trees grow freely in all parts of Gran Canaria and are used extensively for shade as well as for decoration. The cactus-like *Euphorbia canariensis* is a common plant that grows on dry hillsides and could easily be called the 'candlestick plant'. Most of the garden plants will be much more familiar to visitors, especially bougainvillea, seen in a variety of colours, as well as hibiscus and the colourful poinsettia, which grows to the size of a tree on Gran Canaria.

# THE BEST OF GRAN CANARIA

Gran Canaria offers a whole range of fascinating and fun things to see and do across the island. From the natural drama of the mountainous interior to the man-made thrills of its southern theme parks, there are plenty of attractions for all ages and tastes.

## TOP 10 ATTRACTIONS

- **Visit Las Palmas** There is almost too much to see, with the old historical centre, the upmarket shopping streets and the resort beach itself. Two different itineraries are suggested (pages 15 and 23) to make sure you make the most of the capital.

- **Puerto de Mogán** This surely wins the vote for the most attractive – and glamorous – resort on the island (pages 42–5).

- **Visit a theme park** There is a huge selection of theme parks, mostly in the south of the island, which offer entertainment for all the family:
  **Sioux City** (pages 70–71)
  **Mundo Aborigen** (page 59)
  **Parque de Cocodrilos** (pages 69–70)

- **Visit an animal park** See a huge variety of parrots in the beautiful **Palmitos Park** (pages 68–9).

- Have fun in the water at **Aqualand** (page 73).
- **A good night out** There is plenty of nightlife around in the major resorts, but for that special night, why not catch a show at a casino in Las Palmas (page 21), or enjoy barbecue night at Sioux City, and a 'Wild West' show (pages 70–71)?
- **Visit Teror** The old capital (page 54) has fine Canarian wooden balconies and a famous church, Basilica de Nuestra Señora del Pino.
- **Tour the mountainous interior** The high mountains (pages 61–3) offer spectacular scenery unique to the island. Once you have visited the landmarks of Roque Nublo and Roque Bentaiga, you will be able to recognise them from almost anywhere on the island.
- **Camel trekking** No one should leave Gran Canaria without experiencing a camel ride (pages 73–4). There are some great opportunities on this island, and you can trek over sand or ride out to lunch.
- **Top museums** Some of the best include the Museo Casa de Colón in Las Palmas (pages 17–18), the Museo Canario (page 17) and the Casa Museo de los Patrones de la Virgen, in Teror (page 54).

*Roque Bentaiga*

## SYMBOLS KEY

The following symbols are used throughout this book:

address telephone fax website address email

opening times important

The following symbols are used on the maps:

| | |
|---|---|
| information office | city |
| post office | large town |
| shopping | small town |
| airport | point of interest |
| hospital | motorway |
| police station | main road |
| bus station | minor road |
| church | |

numbers denote featured cafés, restaurants & evening venues

### RESTAURANT CATEGORIES

The symbol after the name of each restaurant listed in this guide indicates the price of a typical three-course meal without drinks for one person:

**£** under €20 **££** €20–€40 **£££** over €40

*Maspalomas has extensive sand dunes*

# RESORTS

## Places under the sun

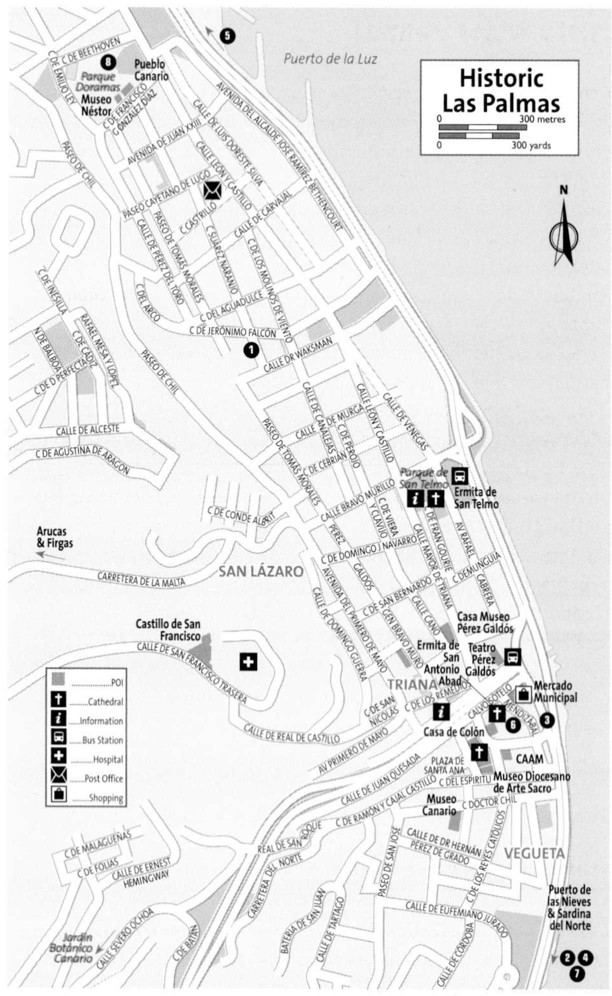
Historic Las Palmas
0 300 metres
0 300 yards
N
Puerto de la Luz
Pueblo Canario
Parque Doramas
Museo Néstor
C DE BEETHOVEN
C DE EMILIO LEY
C DE FRANCISCO G GONZÁLEZ DÍAZ
AVENIDA DE JUAN XXIII
AVENIDA DEL ALCALDE JOSÉ RAMÍREZ BETHENCOURT
CALLE DE LUIS DORESTE SILVA
CALLE LEÓN Y CASTILLO
PASEO DE CHIL
PASEO CAYETANO DE LUGO
C CASTRILLO
CALLE DE CARVAJAL
PASEO DE TOMÁS MORALES
CALLE DE PÉREZ DEL TORO
C SUÁREZ NARANJO
C DE LOS MOLINOS DE VIENTO
C DEL ARCO
C DEL AGUADULCE
C DE JERÓNIMO FALCÓN
CALLE DR WAKSMAN
C DE INESILLA
RAFAEL MESA Y LÓPEZ
C DE CÁDIZ
N DE BALBOA
C DE D PERFECTA
CALLE DE ALCESTE
C DE AGUSTINA DE ARAGÓN
CALLE DE CANALEJAS
CALLE DE MURGA
C DE PEROJO
CALLE LEÓN Y CASTILLO
CALLE DE VENEGAS
C DE CEBRIÁN
Parque de San Telmo
Ermita de San Telmo
C DE CONDE ALBRIT
CALLE BRAVO MURILLO
C DE VIERA Y CLAVIJO
C DE FRAN GOURIE
AV RAFAEL CABRERA
CALLE MAYOR DE TRIANA
Arucas & Firgas
CARRETERA DE LA MALTA
SAN LÁZARO
C DE DOMINGO J NAVARRO
PÉREZ GALDÓS
C DE MUNGUÍA
AVENIDA DEL PRIMERO DE MAYO
CALLE DE DOMINGO GUERRA
C DE SAN BERNARDO
CALLE CANO
GEN BRAVO MURO
Casa Museo Pérez Galdós
Castillo de San Francisco
CALLE DE SAN FRANCISCO TRASERA
Ermita de San Antonio Abad
Teatro Pérez Galdós
TRIANA
C DE LOS REMEDIOS
CALVO SOTELO
MENDIZÁBAL
Mercado Municipal
C DE SAN NICOLÁS
CALLE DE REAL DE CASTILLO
AV PRIMERO DE MAYO
Casa de Colón
POI
Cathedral
Information
Bus Station
Hospital
Post Office
Shopping
CAAM
PLAZA DE SANTA ANA
C DEL ESPÍRITU
Museo Diocesano de Arte Sacro
CALLE DE JUAN QUESADA
C DE RAMÓN Y CAJAL CASTILLO
Museo Canario
C DOCTOR CHIL
REAL DE SAN ROQUE
CALLE DE DR HERNÁN PÉREZ DE GRADO
C DE LOS REYES CATÓLICOS
VEGUETA
C DE MALAGUEÑAS
C DE FOLÍAS
CALLE DE ERNEST HEMINGWAY
CARRETERA DEL NORTE
PASEO DE SAN JOSÉ
BATERÍA DE SAN JUAN
CALLE DE TARTAGO
CALLE DE EUFEMIANO JURADO
CALLE DE CÓRDOBA
Puerto de las Nieves & Sardina del Norte
Jardín Botánico Canario
CALLE SEVERO OCHOA
C DE BATÁN

# Historic Las Palmas

Compact and atmospheric, the Vegueta quarter is where Las Palmas was founded in 1478. Narrow streets overhung with Canarian balconies, the oldest market and the best museums on the island all await discovery. By contrast, the adjoining 16th-century Triana quarter has one of the best shopping streets in the city and a pleasant park.

Allow half a day for this short walk in order to absorb everything of interest along the way. Use the underpass from the bus station to reach Parque de San Telmo. Columbus himself probably set foot on Gran Canaria at this very location, the site of the original port.

Enjoy a coffee in the park at the exquisitely colourful **Kiosk** before making a foray along pedestrianised Calle Mayor de Triana. Take the left fork at the bottom and cross the busy road, the boundary between Triana and Vegueta, into Mendizábal. Pop into the **Mercado Municipal**, open from 08.30 to 13.00, to check out the local produce, turning right up Calle de los Balcones towards the rear of the **Catedral de Santa Ana** and the **Museo Diocesano de Arte Sacro**.

Admire the typical Canarian balconies and – if the door is open – peek into the old courtyard of No 15, just past the **Atlantic Centre of Modern Art**. At the top of this street, the **Casa de Colón's** imposing façade comes into view, its entrance to be found off narrow Calle Colón.

Continue up the right-hand side of the cathedral and bear left into the Plaza de Santa Ana. Check out the town hall here and the bronze dogs in front of the Catedral de Santa Ana, which gave the Canary Islands their name (*canis* is Latin for 'dog'). The route leads to Calle de Doctor Chil and a right turn to No 25, the **Museo Canario**.

## THINGS TO SEE & DO

### Casa Museo Pérez Galdós (Museum House of Pérez Galdós)

The life and work of Canarian-born novelist, playwright and critic Benito Pérez Galdós is reflected in his birthplace here. This attractive

museum contains exhibits of the author's books, furniture that he designed, and a portrait of him by the artist Sorolla. Galdós was very anti-establishment, and branded as a 'rabid anticleric' – a visit to his home would have been looked on as a mortal sin.
ⓐ Calle Cano 6 ⓣ 928 36 69 76 ⓦ www.casamuseoperezgaldos.com
⏲ 09.00–21.00 Mon–Fri, 10.00–18.00 Sat, 10.00–15.00 Sun

**Catedral de Santa Ana (Saint Ana's Cathedral)**
Work began on this cathedral in 1497, but stopped due to a lack of funding and resumed 70 years later. As a result, it is a fascinating mixture of styles, combining a late-Gothic interior and neoclassical exterior. The cathedral contains a fine collection of works of art, including a painting of Christ by Luján Pérez. It can be reached through the **Museo Diocesano de Arte Sacro** (Diocesan Museum of Sacred Art).
ⓐ Plaza de Santa Ana ⓣ 928 33 14 30 ⏲ 10.00–16.30 Mon–Fri, 10.00–13.30 Sat, closed Sun ⓘ Free admission (cathedral); admission charge (museum)

**Centro Atlántico de Arte Moderno – CAAM (Atlantic Centre of Modern Art)**
This beautifully converted white building, on the road behind the Catedral de Santa Ana, is the work of architect Francisco Sáinz de Oiza. He has created a well-balanced gallery behind an 18th-century neoclassical façade. It houses the work of contemporary artists, mainly Canarian and Spanish, and is one of the city's main arts centres.
ⓐ Calle de los Balcones 9–11 ⓣ 928 31 80 76 ⓦ www.caam.net
⏲ 10.00–21.00 Tues–Sat, 10.00–14.00 Sun, closed Mon

**Ermita de San Antonio Abad (Saint Antonio Abad Chapel)**
This 18th-century Baroque church stands on the site of Las Palmas's first church, where Columbus is said to have attended Mass before setting off.
ⓐ Paseo de Mendizàbal 2 ⓘ Entry needs permission from the Cathequist Institute in Dolores Sopeña

## Ermita de San Telmo (Saint Telmo Chapel)

In the Parque de San Telmo, this Canarian church, dedicated to the patron saint of fishermen, was rebuilt in the 17th century following damage by Dutch pirates; the interior is particularly splendid.

ⓐ In the Parque de San Telmo, corner of Calle Bravo Murillo and Avenida Rafael Cabrera ◔ 09.00–14.00 daily

## Jardín Botánico Canario (Canarian Botanic Garden)

To learn more about the wide variety of flora growing on Gran Canaria, it is essential to visit this outstanding botanic garden in the Guiniguada *barranco* (gully) at Tafira Baja. The garden was opened in 1952, and houses many endemic plant species. There are entrances at the top and bottom of the *barranco*, with connecting paths that see you past Canarian palms, some of the ancient trees – the laurasilva – that once covered the whole island, and the cactus house, which contains specimens from all over the world. It's a long climb to the top, and a circular viewing point; suitable refreshment is available beside the top entrance.

ⓐ Tafira Baja is 8 km (5 miles) south of Las Palmas ◔ 09.00–18.00 daily, closed 1 Jan and Good Friday

## Museo Canario (Canarian Museum)

This intriguing collection includes items related to the island's geology. Children will be enthralled by the skulls and mummies, as well as illuminated scale models of cave life that create a fascinating picture of the life of the Aborigens, the original inhabitants of the island.

ⓐ Calle Dr Verneau 2 ⓣ 928 33 68 00 ⓦ www.elmuseocarnario.com ◔ 10.00–20.00 Mon–Fri, 10.00–14.00 Sat & Sun ❗ Admission charge

## Casa de Colón (Columbus Museum)

Here is an opportunity to view the inside of a typical 15th-century Canarian house, built for the island's early governors, where Columbus presented his credentials en route to discovering the New World. On view are exhibits from pre-Columbian America, details about Columbus and his voyages, models of his ships, and displays on the development of the Canaries as a stepping stone to the New World and the origins and history of the city of Las Palmas.

ⓐ Calle Colón 1 ⓣ 928 31 23 73 ⓕ 928 33 11 56 ◷ 09.00–19.00 Mon–Fri, 10.00–17.00 Sat, 09.00–15.00 Sun, closed public holidays

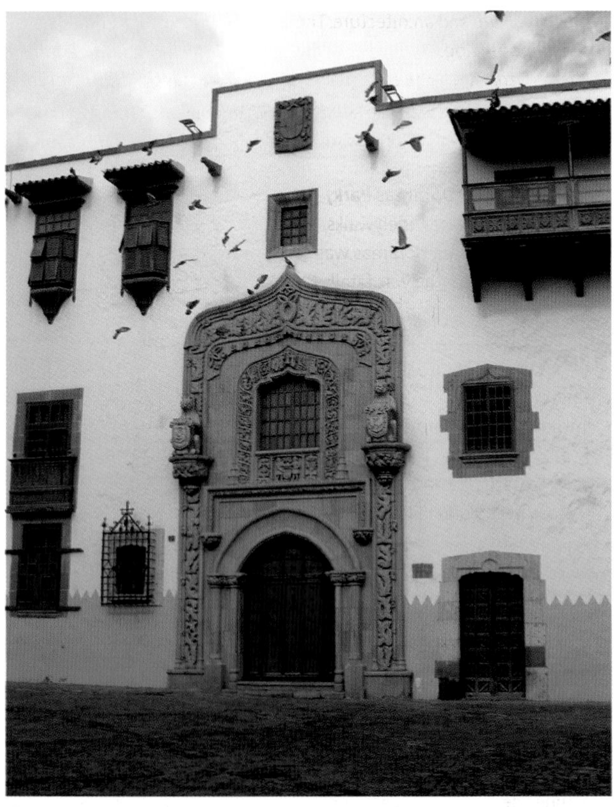

*The Columbus Museum is housed in a typical Canarian building*

### Museo Néstor (Néstor Museum)

This museum houses the life's work of the island's most famous painter, Néstor Martín Fernández de la Torre (1887–1938), who was particularly incensed by the effect of modern development on the island, but had sound ideas for retaining the best of the traditional Canarian culture and architecture. There is folklore dancing here, Sundays 11.00–12.00.

ⓐ Pueblo Canario, on the edge of the Parque Doramas ⓣ 928 24 51 35 ⓕ 928 24 35 76 ◷ 10.00–20.00 Tues–Sat, 10.30–14.30 Sun & public holidays, closed Mon ⓘ Moderate entry fee

### Parque Doramas (Doramas Park)

Parque Doramas has shaded walks, exuberant fountains and a splendid variety of exotic trees. Doramas was the last Aborigen king of Eastern Gran Canaria. In 1481, he was fatally wounded in single combat. The Spanish and Guanche forces then locked in a brief battle, the last act of armed resistance against the Spaniards. Many of Doramas's followers threw themselves from the cliffs, an event commemorated by a sculpture in the garden of the nearby hotel, the Santa Catalina.

ⓐ Barrio de Ciudad Jardín ◷ Daily

### Pueblo Canario (Canarian Village)

This small group of buildings attempts to preserve and re-create the best of Canarian architecture. Designed by Néstor, the buildings were built after his death by his brother. There is an attractive little courtyard with shops selling handicrafts and musical instruments, where you can sit and have a quiet coffee or a bite to eat.

ⓐ The edge of Parque Doramas ⓣ 928 24 29 85 ◷ 10.00–20.00 Tues–Sat, 10.30–14.30 Sun, closed Mon ⓘ Moderate entry fee

### Teatro Pérez Galdós (Pérez Galdós Theatre)

This imposing building was designed by architect Miguel Martín Fernández de la Torre. When first publicised, the new building plans were considered too radical, shocking the island's more conservative

theatregoers. It is now a favourite venue for many of the Las Palmas well-to-do.
ⓐ Plaza Stagno 1 ⓣ 928 43 38 05 ⓦ www.teatroperezgaldos.com

**Vegueta quarter**

Vegueta is the oldest part of Las Palmas, where the Castilian invaders landed in the 15th century, and so it became the powerbase for the ruling classes. It still has a mildly aristocratic air, and contains a number of 17th- and 18th-century mansions with superbly crafted balconies. A casual stroll through this part of historic Las Palmas is well worthwhile.

## TAKING A BREAK

There are many restaurants and cafés in Las Palmas, and tapas bars abound in the narrow side streets just off and north of the Calle Mayor de Triana. Take your time and wander around, but it is a good idea to book if you are looking for that pricier, intimate dinner for two.

**París £–££** ❶ A popular café-bar serving a huge variety of dishes from breakfast till late. ⓐ Plaza de Perón 9 ⓣ 928 23 40 59 ⓛ 08.00–24.00 Mon–Fri, 08.00–22.00 Sat & Sun

**La Fonda de Tafira ££** ❷ Roast meats, good wines and home-made puddings. ⓐ Carretera General del Centro 13–15 ⓣ 928 35 10 91 ⓛ 13.30–16.30, 20.30–24.00 Tues–Sun, closed Mon

**El Herreño ££** ❸ In this popular, old-town restaurant you will find a good selection of tapas, as well as wines from the furthest southwest Canarian island of El Hierro. ⓐ Calle Mendizábal 5–7 ⓣ 928 31 05 13/ 32 20 40 ⓛ 09.30–01.30 daily

**El Pescador ££** ❹ With sea views, this fresh-fish restaurant is a good choice. ⓐ Calle Marina 8 ⓣ 928 33 56 61 ⓛ 12.00–17.00, 20.30–24.00 Tues–Sat, 12.00–17.00 Sun, closed Mon ⓘ Parking area

**Restaurante Churrería Las Arenas ££** ❺ Serves typical Canarian *comidas caseras* (home cooking). ⓐ Centro Comercial Las Arenas ⓣ 928 26 27 67 ◔ 09.00–24.00 daily

**Casa Montesdeoca £££** ❻ This expensive, elegant restaurant in a restored mansion with a lovely courtyard has all the atmosphere, service and food you could hope for in such a charming setting. ⓐ Calle Montesdeoca 10 ⓣ 928 33 34 66 ⓦ www.casamontesdeoca.com ◔ 12.30–16.00, 20.00–24.00 Mon–Sat, closed Sun

**El Cucharón £££** ❼ Famed for producing dishes with a creative spin on traditional Canarian recipes, this air-conditioned restaurant often gets packed. There is access for the mobility impaired. ⓐ Calle Marina 5 ⓣ 928 33 13 65 ◔ 13.00–16.00, 20.00–24.00 Mon–Fri, 20.00–24.00 Sat, closed Sun

## AFTER DARK

There's something for everyone on the night scene of Las Palmas. Parque Santa Catalina is closest to the action, especially that of a more risqué nature, while for the clubbing scene, it's best to seek out posters around the town to find out what is going on, and where. The vogue places are in the Centro Comercial Las Arenas and around the marina, but don't expect too much before 22.00 hours, or to finish before daybreak.

**Gran Casino de Las Palmas** ❽ Sophisticated casino, with French/American Roulette, Black Jack and slot machines, and an international restaurant. ⓐ Hotel Santa Catalina, Parque Doramas ⓣ 928 23 27 91 ◔ 20.00–04.00 Mon–Thur, 20.00–05.00 Fri & Sat, closed Sun; restaurant: 21.00–02.00 Mon–Sat, closed Sun ❗ Men are obliged to wear a jacket and tie and your passport is required for entry

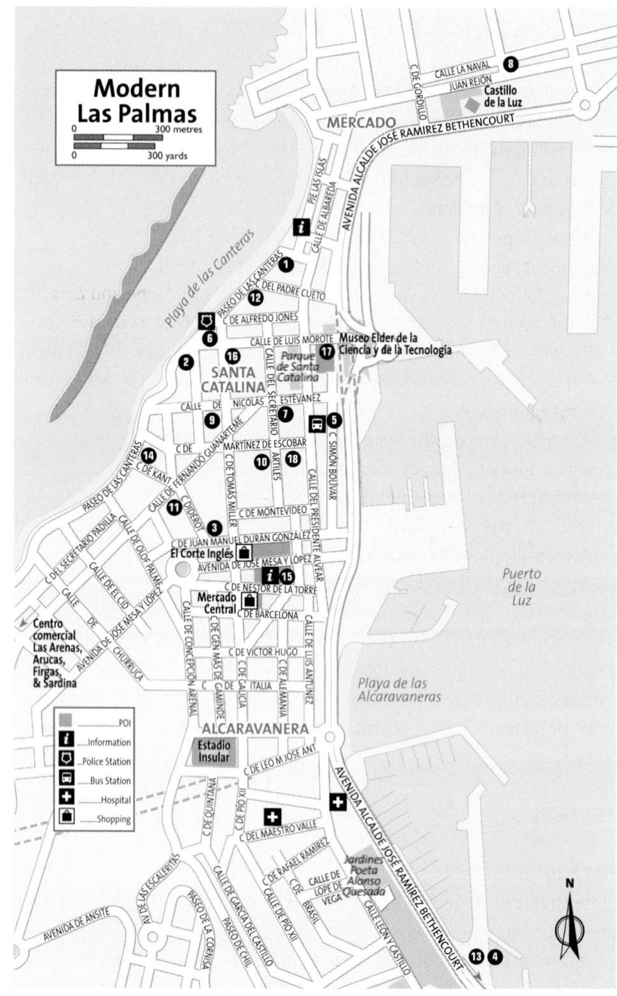
Modern Las Palmas
0
300 metres
0
300 yards
CALLE LA NAVAL
JUAN REJÓN
C DE GORDILLO
Castillo de la Luz
MERCADO
AVENIDA ALCALDE JOSÉ RAMÍREZ BETHENCOURT
PIE LAS ISLAS
CALLE DE ALBAREDA
Playa de las Canteras
PASEO DE LAS CANTERAS
C DEL PADRE CUETO
C DE ALFREDO JONES
CALLE DE LUIS MOROTE
Museo Elder de la Ciencia y de la Tecnología
Parque de Santa Catalina
SANTA CATALINA
CALLE DEL SECRETARIO
CALLE DE NICOLÁS ESTÉVANEZ
C DE MARTÍNEZ DE ESCOBAR
C SIMÓN BOLÍVAR
C DE KANT
CALLE DE FERNANDO GUANARTEME
C DE TOMÁS MILLER
ARTILES
CALLE DEL PRESIDENTE ALVEAR
C DIDEROT
C DE MONTEVIDEO
C DE JUAN MANUEL DURÁN GONZÁLEZ
El Corte Inglés
AVENIDA DE JOSÉ MESA Y LÓPEZ
C DE NÉSTOR DE LA TORRE
Mercado Central
C DE BARCELONA
C DEL SECRETARIO PADILLA
CALLE DE OLOF PALME
CALLE DE EL CID
CALLE DE CHURRUCA
AVENIDA DE JOSÉ MESA Y LÓPEZ
Centro comercial Las Arenas, Arucas, Firgas, & Sardina
CALLE DE CONCEPCIÓN ARENAL
C DE GEN MÁS DE GAMINDE
C DE VÍCTOR HUGO
C DE GALICIA
C DE ALEMANIA
C DE ITALIA
CALLE DE LUIS ANTÚNEZ
Puerto de la Luz
Playa de las Alcaravaneras
ALCARAVANERA
Estadio Insular
C DE LEÓ M JOSÉ ANT
C DE QUINTANA
C DE PÍO XII
C DEL MAESTRO VALLE
C DE RAFAEL RAMÍREZ
C DE BRASIL
CALLE DE LOPE DE VEGA
Jardines Poeta Alonso Quesada
CALLE LEÓN Y CASTILLO
AV DE LAS ESCALERITAS
AVENIDA DE ANSITE
PASEO DE LA CORNISA
PASEO DE CHIL
CALLE DE GARCÍA DEL CASTILLO
CALLE DE PÍO XII
N
POI
Information
Police Station
Bus Station
Hospital
Shopping
1
2
3
4
5
6
7
8
9
10
11
12
13
14
15
16
17
18

# Modern Las Palmas

Shopaholics should head for the Alcaravanera and Santa Catalina quarters of Las Palmas for a sample of just about every shopping experience going. When you reach dropping point, rest at an outside café in Parque Santa Catalina or alternatively you can unwind on the spectacular beach at Playa de las Canteras.

Mesa y López is the hub of a major shopping area where large department stores, including **Marks & Spencer**, rub shoulders with cosmopolitan boutiques, such as **Springfields**, **Bounty**, **Globe** and **Zara**, all flaunting the latest adult fashions. Even infant followers of fashion might be tempted into **OshKosh B'gosh**. Shoe shops, such as **López**, are in plentiful supply and walkers will find **Koronel Tapiocca** a real mecca for walking equipment.

Prominent among the department stores is **El Corte Inglés**, two stores on opposite sides of the road. The store on the north side concentrates on fashions, while the store opposite, in front of the market, sells stationery, books, textiles, electrical goods and photographic equipment. Well worth a quick look is the *mercado* (market), where you can check out the fresh local produce and maybe stock up on some fruit at local prices. Try a *churros con chocolate* (a scrumptious whirl of fried batter dipped into a glass of thick hot chocolate) at **La Habana** on Calle de Barcelona, on the south side of the market. A short walk leads to the Parque de Santa Catalina, where there is a tourist information office open Monday to Friday, from 09.00 to 14.00, as well as more shops and cafés. Playa de las Canteras beach lies only a short distance beyond.

## BEACHES

### Playa de las Canteras

Close to Parque de Santa Catalina, and well supplied with facilities for the visitor, this magnificent strand of golden sand stretches for over 3 km (2 miles). A wide, pedestrianised promenade fringes the beach, a popular playground for the locals and for Spaniards from the mainland.

At the western end of the beach is **Las Arenas (The Sands)** – yet another shopping centre. 10.00–22.00 Mon–Sat, 11.00–14.00 Sun & holidays

## THINGS TO SEE & DO

### Castillo de la Luz (Castle of Light)

At the entrance to the Puerto de la Luz, this large fort was built in the 15th century to defend the bay against pirates.
Juan Rejón 928 44 66 02

### Parque de Santa Catalina (Saint Catalina Park)

Apart from its shady trees and flowerbeds, this park hosts an arts and crafts market on the first Sunday of the month, from 09.00 to 14.30, selling paintings, flowers and decorative arts. A small concert band plays in the square at lunchtime on Sundays.

## EXCURSIONS

### Arucas

This town has been busy making rum ever since sugar cane was introduced to the islands. *Ron Arucas*, as it is known, is widely available, but why not slip into a bar here and try one with a coffee? The town is dominated by the huge church of San Juan Batista, easily the finest piece of architecture on the island, with magnificent stained-glass windows.

### Firgas

Famous for its spring water, which is bottled and sold all over the island, Firgas even has water cascading down the main street over a series of steps. Equally interesting is the street above, where each of the major islands of the Canaries is represented as a pictorial plaque in colourful tiles, complete with a map in relief.

### Puerto de las Nieves

Northwest of the island, you can view remains of the famous Dedo de Dios ('Finger of God'), a slender column of rock just offshore that was destroyed by a storm in 2005. Viewed across a small beach of black sand, it merges against the black cliffs and cannot always be seen instantly.

**Sardina**

This small fishing port is probably the most attractive of the few resorts on the north coast and is a good dive spot. It has a small beach of dark-grey sand and a good selection of bars and restaurants. On a clear day, there is a good view of Tenerife in the distance.

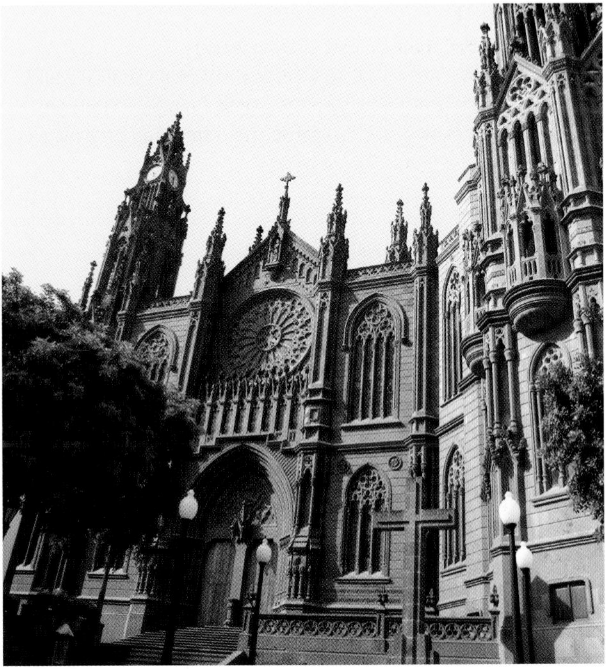

*The façade of San Juan Batista in Arucas*

## TAKING A BREAK

**Al Maccaroni £** ❶ Try this restaurant for Italian pizzas, pasta, fish and meat dishes. ⓐ Paseo de las Canteras 12 ⓣ 928 27 15 80 ❗ Free parking

**El Cerdo Que Rie £** ❷ Inexpensive grill parlour; good food, including flambéed dishes. ⓐ Paseo de las Canteras 31 ⓣ 928 26 36 49

**De Tapa en Tapa £** ❸ Good for a light meal or snack. ⓐ Corner of Calle de Juan Manuel Durán González and Diderot 23 ⓣ 928 49 00 55

**Oh La Lá £–££** ❹ Lively meeting place for a late-night croissant, sandwich or coffee – in fact, lively meeting place any time of the day. ⓐ Avenida Alcalde José Ramírez Bethancourt 18 ⓣ 928 24 14 21 ⓛ 08.00–23.00 Mon–Fri, 09.00–23.00 Sat & Sun

**Tony Roma's £–££** ❺ American chain restaurant famous for its ribs. ⓐ Calle Simón Bolívar ⓣ 928 22 64 00

**El Gallo Feliz ££** ❻ Wide selection of dishes. ⓐ Paseo de las Canteras 35 ⓣ 928 27 17 31

**Restaurante Asador El Cid-Casa Pablo ££** ❼ French Basque place specialising in roast meats and seafood. ⓐ Calle de Nicolás Estévanez 10 ⓣ 928 22 46 31 ⓛ 13.30–16.30, 20.30–24.00 daily

**Restaurante Casa Julio ££** ❽ A range of fish and seafood dishes; roast and grilled meats, too, plus some typical Canarian dishes. ⓐ Calle la Naval 132 ⓣ 928 46 01 39 ⓛ Mon–Sat, closed Sun

**Restaurante El Conejo Alegre ££** ❾ Wines and steaks – house speciality is the *flambeadas* (flambés). ⓐ Calle Joaquín Costa 18 ⓣ 928 26 04 49 ⓛ 13.30–16.30, 20.30–23.30 Tues & Sat, 13.30–16.30 Sun, closed Mon & Wed–Fri

**Tapelia Las Palmas ££** ⓾ An *arrocería* – specialising in rice dishes and Mediterranean cuisine. ⓐ Calle del Secretario Artiles 50 ⓣ 928 27 29 69 ⓛ 13.30–16.30, 20.30–24.00 daily

**Capricho Canario Restaurante £££** ⓫ Canarian gastronomy, served with creative flair. ⓐ Calle Rafael Almeida 34 ⓣ 928 22 72 08 ⓛ 12.00–24.00 Tues–Sun, closed Mon

**Casa Carmelo £££** ⓬ Expensive, but very friendly atmosphere. Excels in grilled meat, or you can choose your own fish. An ideal place for special occasions. ⓐ Paseo de las Canteras 2 ⓣ 928 46 90 56

**La Casa Vasca £££** ⓭ A chance to sample Basque food at its best. ⓐ Avenida Alcalde José Ramírez Bethencourt 18 ⓣ 928 24 18 29 ⓛ Mon–Sat, closed Sun & bank holidays

**El Novillo Precoz £££** ⓮ This place specialises in steak, with beef apparently flown in almost daily from Uruguay! Expensive, but wonderful if you like your meat. ⓐ Calle de Portugal 9 ⓣ 928 22 16 59

## AFTER DARK

**Cuasquias** ⓯ Smart and ideal venue for all ages. Good Latin-American music and top jazz. ⓐ Calle San Pedro 2 ⓣ 928 38 38 40

**Neon Dancing** ⓰ Dancing to an old-fashioned orchestra. ⓐ Calle de Luis Morote 61 ⓣ 928 26 60 79 ⓛ 22.00–05.00 Thur–Sun, closed Mon–Wed

**Pacha Las Palmas** ⓱ A good all-night disco. ⓐ Calle Simón Bolívar 3 ⓣ 928 27 16 84 ⓛ 20.00–04.00 daily

**El Tren** ⓲ A live music bar for a wide range of ages. ⓐ Calle Domingo de Navarro 19 ⓣ 928 36 27 28 ⓛ From 21.00 Mon–Thur, from 22.00 Fri & Sat

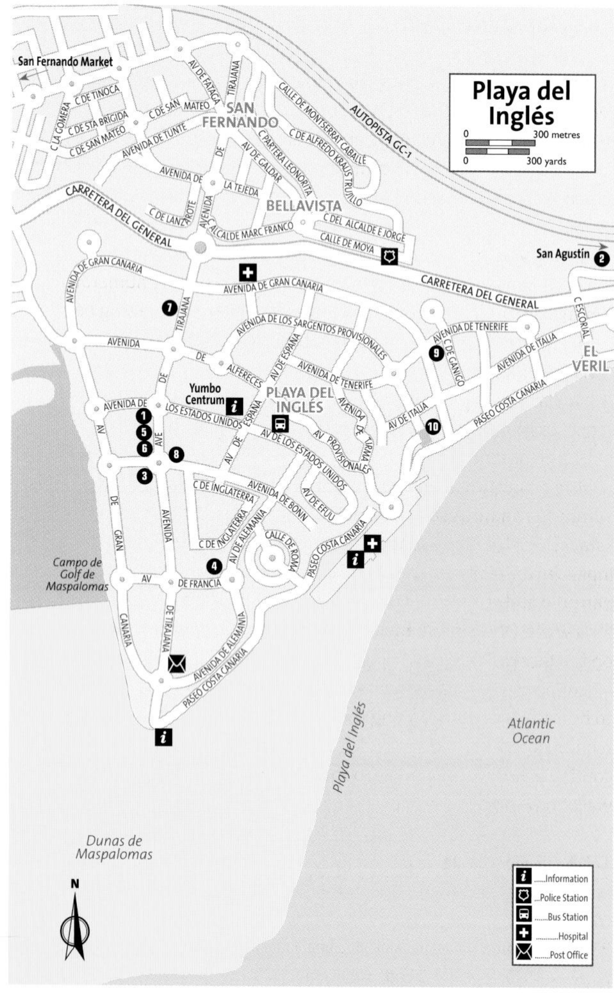
Playa del Inglés
0 300 metres
0 300 yards
San Fernando Market
San Agustín 2
SAN FERNANDO
BELLAVISTA
PLAYA DEL INGLÉS
EL VERIL
AUTOPISTA GC-1
CARRETERA DEL GENERAL
AVENIDA DE GRAN CANARIA
AVENIDA DE LOS SARGENTOS PROVISIONALES
AVENIDA DE TENERIFE
AVENIDA DE ITALIA
PASEO COSTA CANARIA
AVENIDA DE ALFERECES
AVENIDA DE LOS ESTADOS UNIDOS
AV DE ESPAÑA
AV DE TIRAJANA
AV DE FRANCIA
AV DE ALEMANIA
AVENIDA DE ALEMANIA
C DE INGLATERRA
AVENIDA DE BONN
AV DE EFUU
CALLE DE ROMA
AV DE GRAN CANARIA
AV PROVISIONALES
AVENIDA DE TIRMA
C DE GANIGO
C ESCORIAL
CALLE DE MONTSERRAT CABALLÉ
C DE ALFREDO KRAUS TRUJILLO
C PARTERA LEONORITA
AV DE GALDAR
AV DE FATAGA
TIRAJANA
AVENIDA DE TUNTE
AVENIDA DE LA TEJEDA
C DE LANZAROTE
C ALCALDE MARC FRANCO
C DEL ALCALDE E JORGE
CALLE DE MOYA
C LA GOMERA
C DE TINOCA
C DE STA BRIGIDA
C DE SAN MATEO
Yumbo Centrum
Campo de Golf de Maspalomas
Dunas de Maspalomas
Playa del Inglés
Atlantic Ocean
N
Information
Police Station
Bus Station
Hospital
Post Office

# Playa del Inglés

This is where it's at, the place that buzzes through the night, that never seems to want to rest, and that is undoubtedly the island's premier resort. Almost surrounded by sand, it has everything a visitor could wish for. It is well served by public transport, and taxis and car-hire firms are legion. Although there is no obvious centre – no tree-shaded plaza such as you might find in Las Palmas, for example – there is nevertheless a throbbing vibrancy about El Inglés, as it is also known, that more than compensates. Everything happens in or around the numerous commercial centres (*centros comerciales*), which in the evening become lively, animated haunts for disco fanatics, the gay and lesbian community and partygoers.

At Playa del Inglés, sunshine is virtually guaranteed, the beach, which seems to go on forever, is splendid, and the range of facilities and services is second to none.

The nearest thing to a town centre is the sprawling complex of the **Yumbo Centrum**, close by the main tourist office, on Avenida de los Estados Unidos. The Yumbo is the largest of 14 similar centres in Playa del Inglés, all of them vast bazaars of clothes, leather and electronic goods, perfume and souvenirs. If you have the time to slip away from the centre for a while, the **San Fernando market** (see page 30) is by far the largest on the island.

In the evening, as the sun sets and the temperature drops, the place to be is the promenade along the coast, the **Paseo Costa Canaria**, which extends from the beach at San Agustín to Maspalomas and then continues from Maspalomas to Pasito Blanco – not that you need to walk from end to end!

## THINGS TO SEE & DO

### Mini-train

Ride the miniature train, which takes a circular route through town from the El Veril Centre in Avenida de Italia.

**Perla Canaria (Canary Pearl)**

Take a trip to Perla Canaria, where you can choose your own pearls from the oyster tank, and witness the skill of pearl threading. There is a licensed café and a children's play area.

ⓐ On the road to Palmitos Park, bus No 45 runs every 15 min from Playa, bus No 70 runs every 30 min from Puerto Rico ⓣ 928 14 14 64 ⓛ 09.00–19.30 daily ⓘ Free parking, and facilities for visitors with disabilities

**San Fernando market**

Quite apart from the shopping centres (see page 32), the market in Playa del Inglés is the largest on the island, and well worth a visit.

ⓐ Campo Internacional, near Holiday World ⓛ 08.30–13.00 Wed & Sat

## TAKING A BREAK

**Chipi-Chipi £–££** ❶ Good food, well presented. ⓐ Avenida de Tirajana 19 ⓣ 928 76 50 88

**Casa Vieja ££** ❷ This is one of the few typically Canarian restaurants in the resort and it is particularly popular at lunchtime. It has a good atmosphere in the evenings, when the guitarists are busy serenading diners. The menu is well balanced between fish and meat. Why not finish with fresh papaya in liqueur? ⓐ Calle de Fataga 139, San Agustín ⓣ 928 76 90 10

**Las Cumbres ££** ❸ Typical Spanish restaurant, with roast lamb as a tasty speciality. ⓐ Avenida de Tirajana 11 ⓣ 928 76 09 41

**Mi Vaca ££** ❹ International cuisine. ⓐ Avenida de Alemania s/n ⓣ 928 76 80 69 ⓛ 17.00–23.00 Mon–Sat, closed Sun

**Taipei ££** ❺ Good, reasonably priced Chinese. ⓐ Avenida de Tirajana 13 ⓣ 928 76 12 91 ⓛ 13.00–17.00, 19.00–23.00 daily

*Playa del Inglés*

## SHOPPING

This resort's shopping centres seem to have it all, with restaurants and bars, live singers, karaoke and plenty of shops. Here are some of the main centres:

**Aguila Roja** This is the home of several Irish bars and restaurants serving good Irish food. There is plenty of live music around and there are a few gift shops to fill in spare moments.

**Bella Vista** A new commercial centre located behind the Ansoco supermarket in San Fernando.

**CITA** One of the largest, with excellent duty-free shopping, supermarkets and plenty of souvenir shops.

**Gran Chapparal** For a good pub, this is the place to start. Decent British food is also on offer in the bars and restaurants. Satellite television offering live football is a major attraction.

**Kasba** Has the reputation of being the liveliest at night, with many busy bars and restaurants. It is also a good place to buy leather goods, ceramics, duty-free goods and perfumes.

**Metro** Extending to four floors, with a great choice of bars and snack bars scattered among the many shops.

**Plaza Maspalomas** A touch upmarket, with designer clothes, shoe shops, jewellery and perfumeries.

**Yumbo Centrum** This centre is home to the Mardi Gras festival every March. Bars and restaurants here are especially popular with the gay community. Shop here for leather and electrical goods, and souvenirs.

**La Toja ££** ❻ Outstanding fish restaurant. Try *calde de pescado* – fish and vegetable soup. ⓐ Avenida de Tirajana 17 ⓣ 928 76 11 96 ◷ 12.00–16.00, 19.00–24.00 daily

**El Portalón £££** ❼ A smart restaurant with good meat and fish cuisine, and an impressive wine list. ⓐ Avenida de Tirajana 25 ⓣ 928 77 16 22 ◷ 13.00–16.00, 18.30–23.00 daily

**Rias Bajas £££** ❽ A chance to dine in elegant surroundings in one of the more expensive restaurants. Choose from a full international menu or select your own fresh fish from the display in the refrigerated cabinet. ⓐ Edificio Playa del Sol, Avenida de Tirajana ⓣ 928 76 85 48

## AFTER DARK

**Discoteca Joy** ❾ Trendy disco for the under-30s wanting to party the night away. ⓐ Avenida de Gran Canaria ⓣ 928 76 23 99 ◷ 23.00–06.00 daily

**Pachà Playa del Inglés** ❿ Great club, from the same company as the Las Palmas original. ⓐ Avenida de los Sargentos Provisionales 10 ⓣ 928 76 81 77

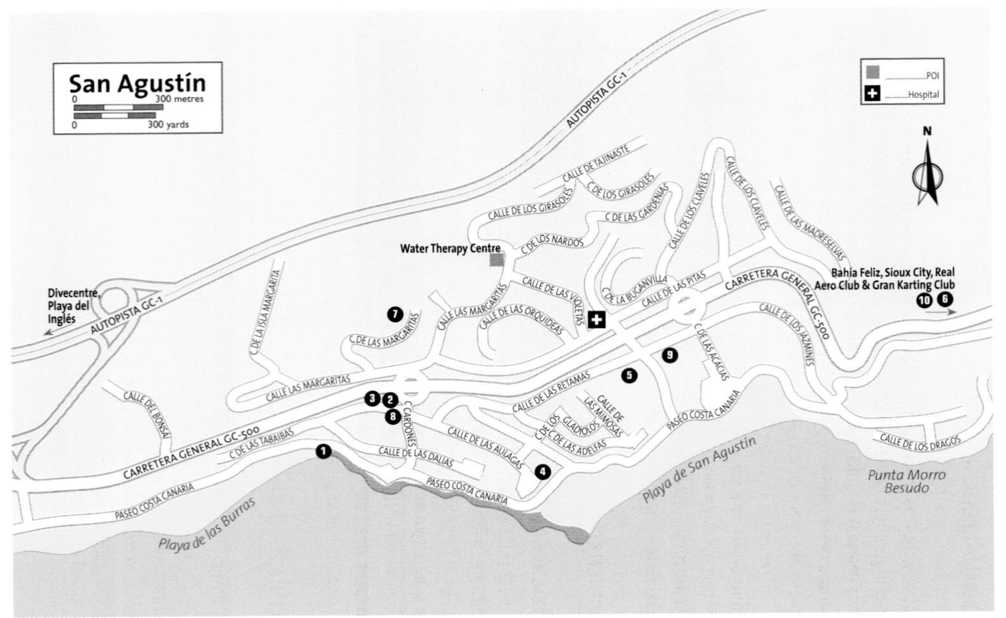

San Agustín
0 300 metres
0 300 yards
POI
Hospital
N
AUTOPISTA GC-1
Water Therapy Centre
Divecentre, Playa del Inglés
Bahía Feliz, Sioux City, Real Aero Club & Gran Karting Club
CALLE DE TAJINASTE
C DE LOS GIRASOLES
CALLE DE LOS GIRASOLES
C DE LAS GARDENIAS
C DE LOS NARDOS
CALLE DE LOS CLAVELES
CALLE DE LAS MADRESELVAS
C DE LA BUGANVILLA
CALLE DE LAS PITAS
CALLE DE LAS VIOLETAS
CALLE LAS MARGARITAS
CALLE DE LAS ORQUIDEAS
C DE LA ISLA MARGARITA
C DE LAS MARGARITAS
CARRETERA GENERAL GC-500
C DE LAS ACACIAS
CALLE DE LOS JAZMINES
CALLE DE LAS RETAMAS
CALLE DE LAS MIMOSAS
C DE LOS GLADIOLOS
C DE LAS ADELFAS
CALLE DE LAS AULAGAS
C CARDONES
CALLE DE LAS DALIAS
CALLE DEL BONSAI
C DE LAS TABAIBAS
PASEO COSTA CANARIA
CALLE DE LOS DRAGOS
Playa de las Burras
Playa de San Agustín
Punta Morro Besudo

# San Agustín

Strangely, this resort, only a short distance away from the action in Playa del Inglés, has never experienced the same mass tourism invasion, and has managed, quite successfully, to maintain an upmarket image. This contrast is highlighted by the fact that it is home to some of the island's most prestigious hotels, including the Melia Tamarindos and its casino.

The resort is in two halves, separated by the No 812 highway, and connected by a series of pedestrian footbridges. Further east is the small resort of Bahía Feliz, a new development of modern bungalows and apartment hotels specifically designed with young, dynamic and well-off clientele in mind.

## BEACHES

The main beach, of dark sand, is the **Playa de San Agustín**, with smaller beaches, the **Playa del Morro Besudo** and the **Playa de las Burras**, on either side. These are the first of the south-coast beaches, and the sands stretch all the way beyond Playa del Inglés to Maspalomas. Sunbeds and parasols can be hired for the day, but there are no watersports here, which means that by comparison it is much quieter and more relaxed. Beachfront cafés along the Playa de las Burras make this the perfect place for the less energetic holidaymaker.

## THINGS TO SEE & DO

### Diving

**Divecentre, PADI Diving School** offers daily diving tuition, underwater trips and some night dives. Transport to and from your hotel and all equipment and insurance is included in the price.

ⓐ Based on board the *Atlantis* in the Pasito Blanco harbour in Maspalomas ⓣ 660 29 18 91 ⓦ www.lgdiving.com

### Flying

Just a short distance northeast of San Agustín is the **Real Aero Club de Gran Canaria**, which offers tandem parachute jumps over the Maspalomas dunes. There is also a good restaurant here. This exhilarating way of seeing the coastline is not for the faint-hearted. You can also book flying lessons here or learn how to free-fall.

ⓐ Carretera General del Sur ⓣ 928 15 71 47 ⓛ Wed–Mon, closed Tues–Sun
ⓘ By appointment only

### Go-karting

The **Gran Karting Club** is the largest in Spain. It provides an ideal variation to the diet of sun, sand and sea.

ⓐ Carretera General del Sur ⓣ 928 15 71 90 ⓕ 928 29 36 71 ⓛ 11.00–22.00 daily (summer); 10.00–21.00 daily (winter)

### Sioux City

This Wild West show, with jail-breaks, shoot-outs, and bows and arrows, is tremendously popular with children (see pages 70–71).

### Water Therapy Centre

This spa is for those of us who love to pamper ourselves. Shouldn't be missed, but not for children.

ⓐ Gloria Palace Hotel, Calle las Margaritas ⓣ 928 76 56 89/77 64 04
ⓕ 928 76 57 46 ⓦ www.gloriapalaceth.com

## TAKING A BREAK

**Boccalino £** ❶ Beachside snack-restaurant, ideal for lunch between sessions in the sun. ⓐ Playa de las Burras ⓣ 928 76 60 18

**Don Quijote £** ❷ Panoramic day- and night-time views over San Agustín from this rooftop bar. ⓐ Centro Comercial ⓣ 928 14 14 24

**Tony's Bar-Grill £–££** ❸ This restaurant offers a varied menu with excellent quality and prices. Centro Comercial

**Chino Canton ££** ❹ Excellent-value Cantonese-style cuisine served in comfortable surroundings. Peking duck has to be ordered 24 hours in advance. Calle de las Aulagas 4–5 928 76 62 30

**Loopys ££** ❺ Sits on a corner where customers can relax and watch the world go by from the terrace area. Specialises in steaks and pizzas, plus kebabs and beef stroganoff. Excellent value and a friendly atmosphere. Calle de las Retamas 928 76 28 92

**Restaurante Los Pescadores ££** ❻ Fresh-fish and seafood restaurant, good value for money. Calle Esquina Bahía Feliz 928 15 71 79 Thur–Tues, closed Wed

**La Gorbea £££** ❼ Elegant restaurant with spectacular panoramic views. Treat yourself to goose-liver pâté, sole with champagne sauce or Chateaubriand. Top floor, Gloria Palace Hotel, Calle de las Margaritas 928 12 85 00

## AFTER DARK

**Riverboat** ❽ Provides a relaxed holiday atmosphere for country-and-western fans, with live music from guest bands, and karaoke. Centro Comercial

**Drago's Bar** ❾ Upmarket cocktail bar within the elegant Hotel Melia Tamarindos. Calle de las Retamas

**Garbo's Dinner Show ££–£££** ❿ For an excellent night out, try this place. Carretera General, Bahía Feliz, Km 44 928 15 70 60 928 15 70 99 19.30–24.00 daily

# Maspalomas

Lying adjacent to Playa del Inglés, Maspalomas is separated from its neighbour only by an extensive system of Sahara-like sand dunes. It is much quieter in character than Playa del Inglés, but boasts a good selection of bars and restaurants. Life revolves around the beach and surrounding shops by day, and includes the Faro 2 shopping centre at night. Visitors looking for a nightlife buzz mostly travel into Playa del Inglés.

Maspalomas is a great place for spending lazy days on the beach, which is a major feature in this resort. It extends eastwards, first to the lagoon, fringed with grasses, and beyond to the extensive sand dunes. These are a great playground in themselves and are a protected area. Behind part of the beach lies the **Paseo de Faro**, full of bars, cafés and souvenir shops, where you can find anything from a cool beer or a light snack to a full meal.

The **faro**, or lighthouse, is a significant landmark lying on the western side of the resort. Further west lies another beach, the **Playa de la Mujer**. This beach occupies a corner too breezy for sunbathers, but the rough seas and windy conditions are favoured by board and windsurfers.

Further west still is **Pasito Blanco**; accessible from the main highway, the public may walk down to this small, private spot. It provides access to the more sheltered end of the Playa de la Mujer, where those who seek a little peace and quiet in order to sunbathe nude may find it.

Inland from Pasito Blanco, off to the right on the GC812 going from Maspalomas to Mogán, is a recently opened outdoor activity club, for trekking and mountain-bike rental, but only for organised groups.

Three 18-hole golf courses are worth visiting in the area. Lying behind the sand dunes is the excellent **Campo de Golf** (ⓐ Avenida Neckermann ⓣ 928 76 25 81). The restaurant overlooking the course is open to the general public (see page 41). In the mountains behind Pasito Blanco, off the GCI, 6 km (4 miles) west of Maspalomas, is **Salobre Golf** (ⓣ 928 01 01 03 ⓦ www.salobregolfresort.com ⓔ reservation@salobregolfresort.com), which has two 18-hole golf courses.

## THINGS TO SEE & DO

### Camel riding in the dunes

Take a camel trek through the famous Maspalomas dunes and imagine you are in the Sahara.

### Dune trekking

It is easier to walk back from Playa del Inglés to Maspalomas, using the lighthouse as a guide, than the other way round. From the end of the access road through the Riu Palace Hotel, at the end of Avenida de Tirajana in Playa del Inglés, it is possible to see the lighthouse in Maspalomas. Use it to navigate by as you trek across the dunes – not

*The dunes of Maspalomas*

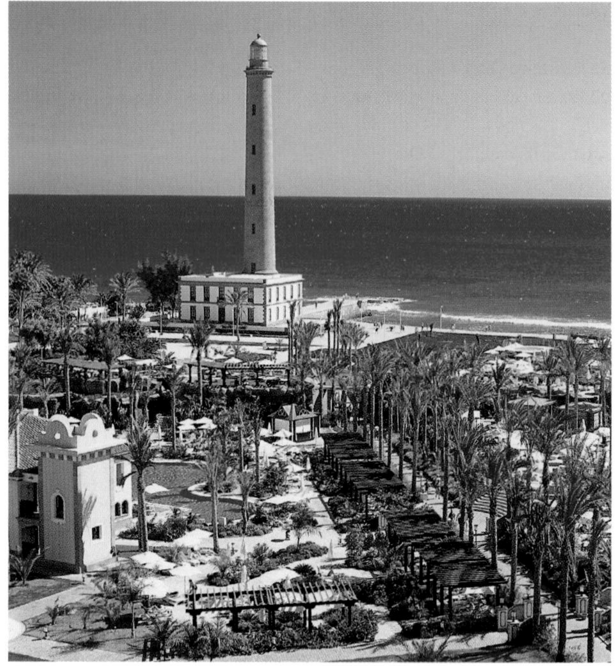

*Maspalomas is dominated by its lighthouse*

recommended after a late night in a bar, but good for some stimulating exercise the next day. Walking across sand is far from easy and will give you aching calves – allow an hour and 30 minutes for the walk.

**Sky diving**

A 20-minute flight over Gran Canaria, then free-falling for 45 seconds before opening your parachute.

t 928 15 73 25 w www.skydivegrancanaria.es

## TAKING A BREAK

**Restaurante Canton Faro £–££** Chinese restaurant with excellent-value good food. ⓐ Lugar las Meloneras ⓣ 928 14 36 99 ◷ 12.00–23.00 daily

**Altstadt Düsseldorf ££** Offering excellent views, with a full international menu. After a shrimps-in-garlic starter, you could try the Chateaubriand. ⓐ Avenida de Francia 1 ⓣ 928 76 26 30

**Broncemar 2 ££** This restaurant is especially famous for its steaks, but you can just as easily choose the grilled lobster from the seafood section or the chicken from the general list. ⓐ Ground floor, Centro comercial Faro 2 ⓣ 928 76 89 87 ◷ 10.00–23.00 daily

**Campo de Golf ££** Enjoy views over the fairways in this comfortable but formal atmosphere. The menu is varied, so if the German sausage is not for you, select from the pizza list or go for a peppered sirloin. ⓐ Avenida Neckermann ⓣ 928 76 80 26 ◷ 08.00–21.00 Mon–Sat, 10.00–17.00 Sun

## AFTER DARK

**Piano Beach Bar** A very relaxed atmosphere greets visitors to this upmarket bar, where the pianist plays nightly. There is additional entertainment on some nights. ⓐ Paseo del Faro

### SHOPPING

**Arguineguin Market** Tuesday is market day in Arguineguin, west of Maspalomas, with souvenirs, T-shirts, clothing, African woodcarvings and fresh fruit on offer. The harbour, too, is interesting, especially when fresh fish are being unloaded.

**Centro comercial Faro 2** Circular in design and built on two floors, this major attraction has a slightly upmarket air, not only in the style and appearance, but also in the goods on display.

# Puerto de Mogán

Puerto de Mogán easily wins the accolade of being the most charming port on the island, with the added bonus that a visit here can make you feel like a millionaire. One of the greatest pleasures in this smart marina is spotting luxury yachts and pretending that they belong to you, or trying to guess which rich and famous people they might really belong to.

Unlike most other resorts in the south, Puerto de Mogán has a history, and started out as a fishing village serving the needs of inland Mogán. With the growing demands of tourism, it has developed into a marina – and while the fishermen's cottages have been preserved, they are not in their original form. Now little remains of the old character, and the town has effectively been converted into a model village.

Neat, uniform rows of old cottages now look freshly made from confectioner's icing sugar and as white as the virgin snow. Hand-painted borders around doors and windows – in pastel ochre, deep green or soft purple – make each new house encountered different from its neighbour. The final drapes of scarlet bougainvillea tumbling from wrought-iron balconies, with borders of peach-coloured hibiscus, create a picture that is as refreshing as it is unexpected. Small, arched bridges, crossing waterways and connecting houses, emphasise the Lilliputian scale and lend the resort a pleasing touch of Venice.

Puerto de Mogán has an atmosphere best enjoyed at leisure. It is a place for strolling, enjoying the marina activities and watching the fishermen arrive with their catch. There are plenty of waterside cafés and bars to sit in while reflecting on life and watching the world at play.

## BEACHES

There is a good-sized beach of grey sand adjacent to the marina at Puerto de Mogán. The drab colour of the sand makes the beach look uninspiring, but it is as comfortable as any other – although, since dark colours absorb heat, it can get a little hotter in the sun. The beach is well sheltered and there are sunbeds for hire, as well as waterskiing facilities.

## THINGS TO SEE & DO

### Diving aboard the *Yellow Submarine*

A thrilling trip to the bottom of the sea on the *Yellow Submarine* starts here in Puerto de Mogán. This vessel was commissioned in 1988 and built in Finland especially for observing marine life. The journey beneath the high seas lasts around 45 minutes. There are free buses that depart from many hotels at various times. For more information, ask your holiday representative or your hotel.

ⓣ 928 56 51 08 ⓕ 928 56 50 48 ◷ 09.00–19.00 Mon–Fri, 10.00–17.00 Sat & Sun

## EXCURSIONS

### Mogán

Mogán village lies 12 km (7 miles) inland, up one of the most fertile and beautiful valleys on the island. It is easy to head to Mogán for lunch on bus No 84, but keep an eye on the return times. Riding up the valley, you will pass crops of aubergines, papayas, avocados and coffee beans, which eventually give way to the green pastures of the upper valley. Mogán itself is a small, fairly typical Canarian mountain village that has adapted to greeting tourists riding up from the port. Terraces by the church and town hall provide good picnic places. There are some good restaurants lining the main road.

## TAKING A BREAK

There are several reasonable places to eat and drink, but most of the restaurants around the harbour are expensive. For better value, at the cost of losing the beautiful views, try to find somewhere away from the harbourfront.

**El Alamo ££** You can enjoy your meal on the panoramic terrace. The menu includes traditional Canarian rabbit or goat in garlic sauce, and it won't break the bank. ⓐ Calle San José 11, Mogán ⓣ 928 56 95 93

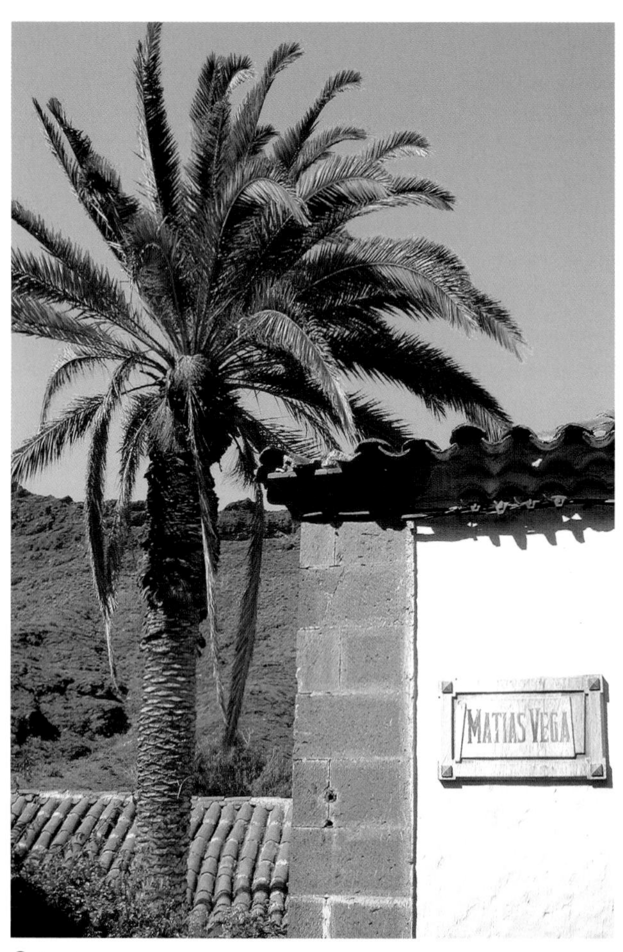


Mogán

**SHOPPING**
Friday is market day in Puerto de Mogán, when the large market spreads over vast areas of the car park, the rear of the beach and the adjacent streets. Lace tablecloths, leather goods, clothing, African carvings and souvenirs can be found in abundance here.

**El Castillete ££** This snack bar offers a fairly standard menu at reasonable prices. The lunchtime set menu is good value. ⓐ Esplanada del Castillete ⓣ 928 56 54 68 ⓛ 10.00–22.00 daily

**Tu Casa ££** Reasonably priced restaurant specialising in fish; try the *parrillada de pescado* (mixed grill of fish). ⓐ Avenida de las Artes 18 ⓣ 928 56 50 78 ⓛ 11.00–23.00 daily

**Mesón Patio Canario II ££–£££** Attractive restaurant with good regional fish dishes, but it is rather pricey. Try the spiny lobster casserole or grilled stone bass. ⓐ Esplanada del Castillete (Patio Canaria) ⓣ 928 56 52 74

**El Faro £££** This rather expensive restaurant is set around the base of the lighthouse at the end of the harbour quay. The menu is fully international and very extensive. Daytime snacks are also available here at very reasonable prices. ⓐ Puerto de Mogán Marina ⓣ 928 56 52 85 ⓛ 10.00–23.00 daily

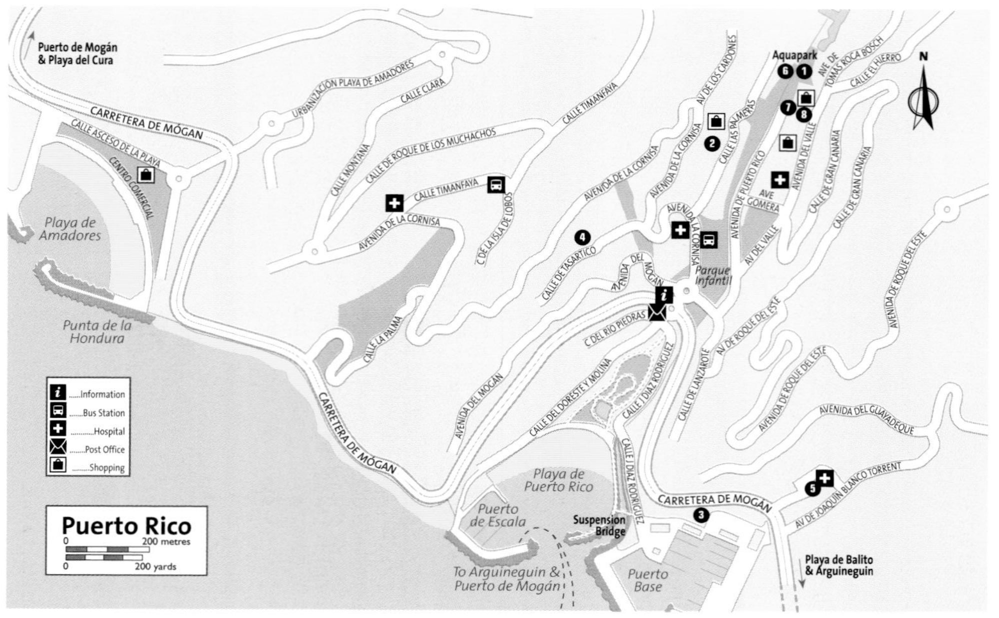
Puerto de Mogán & Playa del Cura
CARRETERA DE MÓGAN
CALLE ASCESO DE LA PLAYA
CENTRO COMERCIAL
Playa de Amadores
Punta de la Hondura
URBANIZACIÓN PLAYA DE AMADORES
CALLE CLARA
CALLE MONTAÑA
CALLE DE ROQUE DE LOS MUCHACHOS
CALLE TIMANFAYA
AVENIDA DE LA CORNISA
C DE LA ISLA DE LOBOS
CALLE LA PALMA
CALLE DE TASARTICO
AVENIDA DEL MOGÁN
C DEL RIO PIEDRAS
CALLE DEL DORESTE Y MOLINA
CALLE J DIAZ RODRIGUEZ
AV DE LOS CARDONES
CALLE LAS PALMERAS
AVENIDA LA CORNISA
Parque Infantil
AVENIDA DE PUERTO RICO
AVE GOMERA
AV DEL VALLE
AVENIDA DEL VALLE
Aquapark
AVE DE TOMAS ROCA BOSCH
CALLE EL HIERRO
CALLE DE GRAN CANARIA
N
CALLE DE LANZAROTE
AV DE ROQUE DEL ESTE
AVENIDA DE ROQUE DEL ESTE
AVENIDA DEL GUAYADEQUE
AV DE JOAQUIN BLANCO TORRENT
CARRETERA DE MOGÁN
Playa de Puerto Rico
Puerto de Escala
Suspension Bridge
To Arguineguin & Puerto de Mogán
Puerto Base
Playa de Balito & Arguineguin
Information
Bus Station
Hospital
Post Office
Shopping
Puerto Rico
0 200 metres
0 200 yards

# Puerto Rico

Puerto Rico is a compact and picturesque resort, which surrounds a very attractive, family-oriented beach of dark golden sand. There is a good centre for watersports on one side of the beach and a busy marina on the other. The rest of the resort tiers loftily up the hillsides that surround Puerto Rico like an amphitheatre.

## BEACHES

The focal point of this resort is the naturally sheltered beach. Further protection is provided by enclosing piers, which calm the seas to make a safe beach for children. It is also great for watersports (see page 49), but these take place outside the bay.

Participants are marshalled in and out and swimmers are protected by a roped-off area. The shallow seas within the bay are greatly enjoyed,

*Playa de Amadores lies in a sheltered bay*

particularly by young children. Sunloungers and umbrellas are available for hire, with good drinks and snacks facilities at the rear of the beach.

Although the beach is a good size, it can still be crowded. The pier enclosing the beach on the marina side is lined with sunbeds. It is ideal for those who like to sunbathe without getting sand between the toes. A **rope suspension bridge** over the river here gives access to Calle Juan Diaz Rodriguez and the marina itself.

Bustling at the best of times, this marina is the starting point for a whole variety of sailing excursions. The *Líneas Salmón* ferry offers regular sailings to neighbouring ports (see below and opposite), and departs from here.

The rocky coastline between Arguineguin and Puerto de Mogán offers few opportunities to sunbathe, but where it does, new, smaller and decidedly quieter resorts develop. Two such beaches – definitely worth going that bit further for – are the **Playa de Balito** and the **Playa del Cura**.

Heading 5 km (3 miles) west from Puerto Rico towards Mogán, there is a beautiful, man-made beach called **Playa de Amadores**. It is very safe for swimming and has every amenity: showers, toilets, cafés and restaurants.

## THINGS TO SEE & DO

### Arguineguin by boat

The *Líneas Salmón* in Puerto Rico runs trips to Arguineguin for the market. ⓐ Puerto Rico harbour ⓛ First departure is at 10.30, daily, and then every two hours until 16.30

### SHOPPING

There are three large shopping centres (*centros comerciales*) in the resort. The biggest of them is the **Centro comercial Puerto Rico** on Avenida Tomás Roca Bosch. The other two are **Europa** and **Playa de Amadores** (on the beach of the same name). Each has a range of shops selling duty-free goods, electrical items, perfumes, aftershaves and souvenirs. Lladró pottery is available from a shop in Puerto Rico shopping centre.

## Diving

The **Aquanauts Dive Centre** offers a chance to descend into a new world, with daily dives. Night dives are also available, plus full-day dives and introductory courses for beginners.

ⓐ On the beach front at Puerto Rico ⓣ 928 56 06 55 ⓦ www.aquanauts-divecenter.com

## Ferry to Puerto de Mogán

*Líneas Salmón* sails from Puerto Rico harbour to Puerto de Mogán (pages 42–5). ⓣ 928 24 37 08/649 91 93 83/649 92 59 18 ⓗ Sails hourly from 10.00 to 17.00 daily; return times are 45 minutes later than departure times ⓘ Single or return tickets can be purchased on board for €10 return, or €6 single at the time of writing

## Sailing

For anyone who is staying in Puerto Rico for two weeks and whose children have a desire to learn how to sail, the 13-day summer sailing course, the **Escuela de Vela Joaquín Blanco Torrent**, is specifically targeted at 8- to 15-year-olds, and includes theory and practice. Course pupils do get time off for other sports like football and volleyball.

ⓐ Calle Olímpicos Doreste y Molina ⓣ 928 56 07 72 ⓘ Bookings can be made via the Federación Canaria de la Vela

## Taking to the water

Puerto Rico is a great centre for watersports. Here you can paddle out gently on a pedalo; windsurfing is also available and experienced sailors can hire a sailing boat. All these facilities are available from the western side of the beach.

## TAKING A BREAK

**Los Danieles £** ❶ This is a much-frequented bar/café. If you want a snack, this is the place to go. ⓐ Centro comercial Puerto Rico ⓣ 928 56 04 15 ⓗ 08.00–23.30 Mon–Sat, closed Sun

**Osaka £** ❷ Chinese, Indonesian and Japanese meals. ⓐ Centro comercial Europa ⓣ 928 56 13 84 ◷ 16.30–24.00 daily

**Don Quijote ££** ❸ This restaurant offers an extensive menu, especially the starters, which include a tapas selection. From frog's legs or buttered French beans with ham, you could move on to quails in red wine or settle for a good steak. The special lunchtime Terrace Menu is very good value. ⓐ Edificio Porto Novo ⓣ 928 56 09 01 ◷ Sept–7 June

**Pancho Villa Restaurante ££** ❹ Tex-Mex food and Latin American music. ⓐ Calle de Tasartico 17 ⓣ 928 56 05 29

**Restaurant El Gaitero ££** ❺ On the way into the resort, this first-floor restaurant specialises in regional Galician dishes. ⓐ Barranco Agua la Perra ⓣ 928 56 20 44 ◷ 13.00–01.00 daily

**The Winston Churchill ££** ❻ Caters in British and Indian food, offering good-value meals, from cottage pie and sirloin steaks to balti or tikka masala. Caters well for children. ⓐ Centro comercial Puerto Rico 30–31 ⓣ 928 56 15 26 ◷ Tues–Sun, closed Mon

**Big Horn Steak House ££–£££** ❼ For something rather more upmarket – but be prepared to pay a little more. It specialises in steak dishes and has a very tempting menu. Children can choose from their own menu. ⓐ Centro comercial Puerto Rico ⓣ 928 56 19 03 ◷ 18.30–23.00 daily

## AFTER DARK

**Disco Joker** ❽ Popular with under 30s. Music from the charts gives way to dance music as the night wears on. ⓐ Basement, Centro comercial Puerto Rico ⓣ 928 56 20 05 ◷ 23.00–07.00 daily ❗ Free before 01.00

▶ *Visitors can relish stunning views across the island*

# EXCURSIONS

Out & about

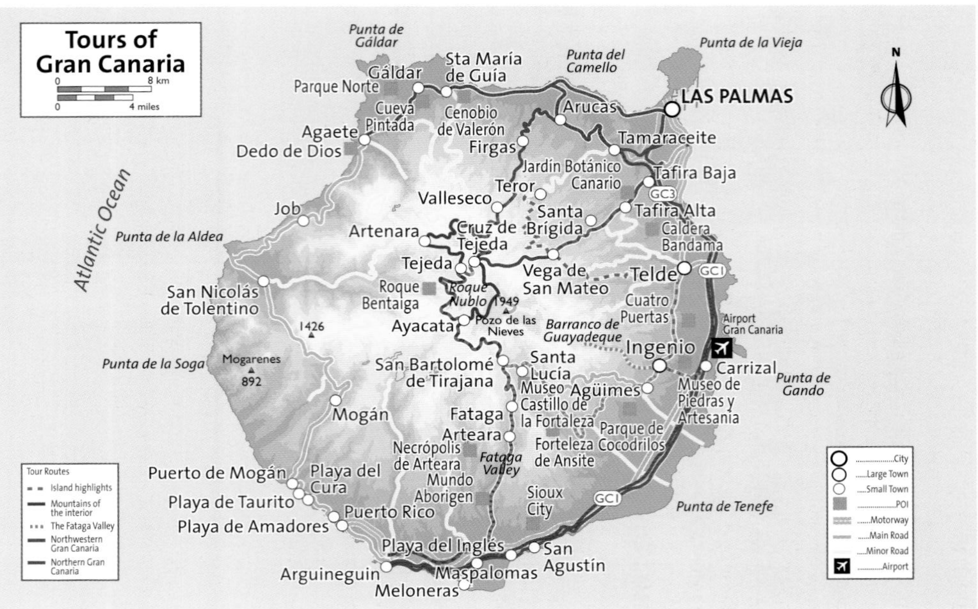
Tours of Gran Canaria
0 8 km
0 4 miles
Punta de Gáldar
Sta María de Guía
Punta del Camello
Punta de la Vieja
N
Parque Norte
Gáldar
LAS PALMAS
Cueva Pintada
Cenobio de Valerón
Arucas
Agaete
Dedo de Dios
Firgas
Tamaraceite
Jardín Botánico Canario
Tafira Baja
Teror
GC3
Atlantic Ocean
Valleseco
Santa Brígida
Tafira Alta
Job
Cruz de Tejeda
Caldera Bandama
Punta de la Aldea
Artenara
Tejeda
Vega de San Mateo
Telde
GC1
San Nicolás de Tolentino
Roque Bentaiga
Roque Nublo
1949
Cuatro Puertas
Airport Gran Canaria
1426
Ayacata
Pozo de las Nieves
Barranco de Guayadeque
Ingenio
Punta de la Soga
Mogarenes
892
San Bartolomé de Tirajana
Santa Lucía
Carrizal
Punta de Gando
Museo Agüimes
Museo de Piedras y Artesanía
Castillo de la Fortaleza
Mogán
Fataga
Arteara
Parque de Cocodrilos
Necrópolis de Arteara
Fataga Valley
Forteleza de Ansite
Tour Routes
Island highlights
Mountains of the interior
The Fataga Valley
Northwestern Gran Canaria
Northern Gran Canaria
Puerto de Mogán
Playa del Cura
Mundo Aborigen
Sioux City
Punta de Tenefe
Playa de Taurito
Puerto Rico
Playa de Amadores
Playa del Inglés
San Agustín
Arguineguin
Maspalomas
Meloneras
City
Large Town
Small Town
POI
Motorway
Main Road
Minor Road
Airport

# Island highlights tour

This long day trip (192 km/120 miles) offers a rich mix of lowland and mountain scenery with a few well-chosen stopping places, beginning and ending at Playa del Inglés (see pages 29–33). The weekend is the best time for this trip because there is a big local market in Teror, one of the best on the island. It starts up on Saturday and is in full swing by Sunday. Watch out for the special breads on sale here, such as *pan de huevo* (egg bread), *milo* (corn bread), *ajo* (garlic bread) and *leche, pasas y almendras* (milk, raisin and almond bread).

## THE ROUTE

From Playa del Inglés, head off in the direction of Las Palmas on the GC1. Leave at the Carrizal junction and take the road to Ingenio. Turn right at the lights in Ingenio on to the unsigned but main road to Telde. Look for the Museo de Piedras y Artesanía on the right very soon after.

### Museo de Piedras y Artesanía (Museum of Rocks and Crafts)

The displays here cover a curious mixture of lace, bric-a-brac, Canarian bedroom furniture, rocks and corals, not to mention a small chapel and a parrot in a cage! As much as anything else, it is also a shop, so there is a chance to buy lace (especially tablecloths), leather goods and jewellery.

08.00–18.30 Mon–Sat, closed Sun

Further on, just before joining the main road to Telde, is a sign for **Cuatro Puertas**, an ancient sacred site. Negotiate Telde using the eastern bypass, and, immediately beyond the last roundabout, turn left to Caldera Bandama to view the crater.

### Caldera Bandama (Bandama Cauldron)

This requires only a brief stop to inspect the perfectly formed volcanic crater. A farm nestles 200 m (656 ft) down on the bottom, surviving on the fertility of the weathered volcanic soil. The route now leads to Tafira Alta, Santa Brígida and on to Vega de San Mateo.

**Vega de San Mateo**

There is a good market here at weekends, with fresh fruit and vegetables, home-grown herbs and local cheeses and wines. (See also page 82.)

In Vega de San Mateo, turn right to travel north to Teror.

**Teror**

Teror was once the island capital, and architecturally it is the finest Canarian town on the island. Wooden balconies are a feature of old Canarian houses and there are plenty to see in Teror. There is hardly any need to walk further than the street facing the **Basilica de Nuestra Señora del Pino** to see a good selection.

The basilica is dedicated to the Virgin of the Pines, the patron saint of Gran Canaria. The legend is that, in 1481, the Virgin Mary appeared on the branch of a pine tree before the village priest. A simple church was built on the site in 1515 and there has been a church there ever since. Now greatly modified, the present building has an impressive baroque façade, while inside there is a coffered ceiling and some fine carving. Catching the eye most of all is the richly decorated statue of the Madonna, set in the high altar, sumptuously adorned in gold, silver and precious stones.

Located across the road adjacent to the church entrance is the **Casa Museo de los Patrones de la Virgen**, a fine old traditional Canarian house belonging to the aristocratic Manrique de la Lara family. It is now open as a museum. The entrance leads first into a shady inner courtyard with fine wooden balconies. From here there is access to the various rooms, all still furnished in the old style. Horse-drawn carriages, sedan chairs and a 1951 Triumph Renown are garaged in the rear courtyard.

Leave Teror on the Firgas road, but climb through Valleseco, eventually reaching Cruz de Tejeda.

### Cruz de Tejeda & Roque Nublo

Located high in the mountains at an altitude of nearly 1,490 m (4,890 ft), Cruz de Tejeda is regarded as the centre of the island. It is something of a crossroads, where traders used to set up stalls to catch the passing trade. A stone cross stands in front of the main building, the Parador Nacional de Tejeda. From here you can see a view of the island's most famous landmark, **Roque Nublo** (see page 63). The Parque Rural del Nublo at Tejeda, as the area is known, has been designated as a protected biosphere by UNESCO.

On the way to Tejeda, watch out for further views of the rocky landmarks of Roque Nublo, El Fraile and Roque Bentaiga. Winding roads are a feature of mountain driving on Gran Canaria and there are several on this section.

From Tejeda, head towards San Bartolomé de Tirajana and then back to Playa del Inglés along the beautiful Fataga Valley (see page 64). Watch out for an excellent viewpoint once through Fataga and out of the valley.

## TAKING A BREAK

On the way to the Parque Rural del Nublo, you pass through Artenara village, which has some good places to eat (see also page 63):

**Las Perdiz £** The owner, Antonio, is very friendly and the menu is varied and good value. ⓐ Opposite the petrol station ⓣ 928 66 60 71 ⓛ 12.00–late Tues–Sun, closed Mon

On the northeast side of Vega de San Mateo, on the road from Santa Brigida, try:

**La Veguetilla ££** A well-known local meeting place, with good service and a bit of class. It specialises in meat dishes. ⓐ Calle Veguetilla 49 ⓣ 928 66 07 64 ⓛ 13.00–17.00 Tues–Thur & Sun, 20.00–24.00 Fri & Sat, closed Mon

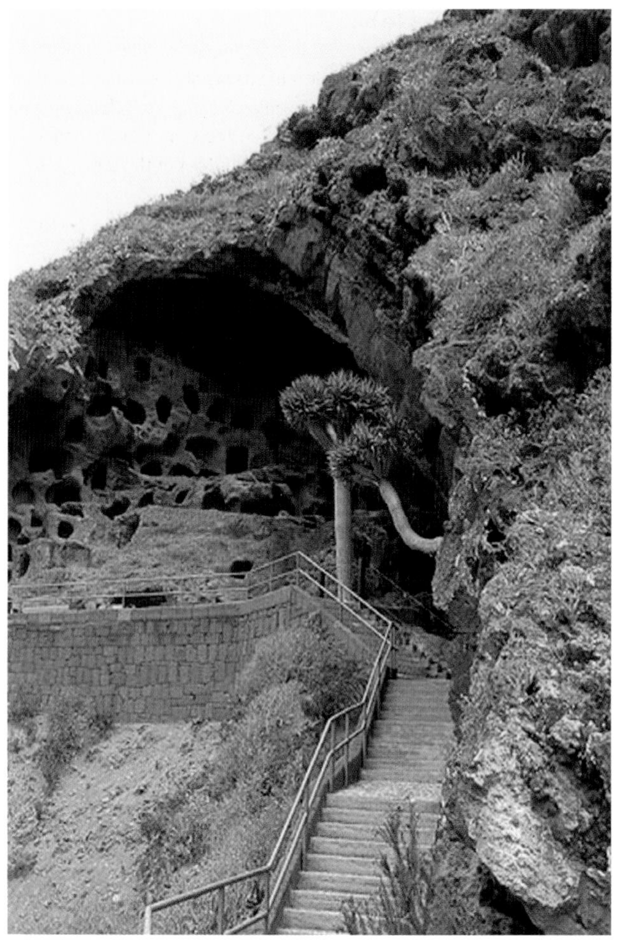

The entrance of the Cenobio de Valerón

# The Aborigen trail

The Aborigens were the pre-Hispanic inhabitants of the Canary Islands, the people who lived here before the Spaniards started to colonise the islands early in the 15th century. They are also known as the Guanches (pronounced 'Wanches'), particularly so on Tenerife, but the term Aborigens is mostly favoured on Gran Canaria.

The remains and artefacts of the Aborigen culture are richer on this island than on any other in the Canaries. The original people of Gran Canaria lived with little or no interference until the Spaniards arrived. While the rest of Europe developed advanced skills in building, engineering and science, the Aborigens lived a primitive life, had no navigational skills and had not discovered metal. They lived largely in caves – the island's geology led to an abundance of such shelters – but they had the skills to build houses from stone. Exhibits at Roque Bentaiga show how this ridge was inhabited by the Aborigens (see page 61).

There are strong connections in language and habits between the Aborigens and the ancient Berbers of North Africa. It is therefore possible that they may have arrived from Africa as migrants or invaders, probably around the 2nd or 1st century BC. Two kingdoms existed on the island, centred around Telde and Gáldar. A hierarchical system existed within Aborigen society, with a class of nobles supporting the king. Peasants made up the largest class and they were in charge of farming, herding and manufacturing. Haircuts, beards and dress were often used as symbols to denote class.

## THINGS TO SEE & DO

### Necrópolis de Arteara (Arteara Necropolis)

Adjacent to Arteara, just north of Playa del Inglés, is a genuine Aborigen necropolis, or cemetery, which has only recently been afforded the recognition and protection it deserves. To reach it, walk through the village to the far side, where there is a sign for the necropolis. Take the

small path to the left of the sign, which leads to the gate of the fenced enclosure. Enter through the unlocked gate and follow the path. Look uphill to the right to pick out the stone-built burial tombs. They blend in so well that they are initially difficult to see, but there are a good number around.

ⓐ On the No 18 bus route between Playa del Inglés and Fataga

🕒 Daily

**Cenobio de Valerón (Convent of Valerón)**

Located in the north of the island, near Gáldar, this honeycomb of caves in the rock face is part of Guanche history. The site is beset with tales and intrigue. The romantic will be happy to believe that this is where the 15-year-old daughters of Guanche nobility were prepared for marriage. It was believed that women with wide hips and full breasts delivered healthy children, so the girls were fed well. Others believe these caves were nothing more than a grain store. Steps lead up to the site where the keeper has trained the local lizards to feed from his hand. (See also page 77.)

*Mundo Aborigen shows scenes of everyday life*

## Cueva Pintada (Painted Cave)

Signposted from Gáldar, the Cueva Pintada contains the only remaining wall paintings in the Canaries. These paintings are also reproduced in the Museo Canario (see page 17).

## Forteleza de Ansite (Ansite Fort)

Located near Santa Lucía, in the centre of the island, the Forteleza (see page 66) is not actually a fortress, as the name suggests, but an outcrop of rock resembling a fortress. This was the final battleground in the Spanish campaign to conquer the island in 1483, where resistance by the Aborigens finally crumbled. A memorial celebration takes place here every year on 29 April.

## Mundo Aborigen (Aborigens' World)

Occupying a fairly large site, Mundo Aborigen, which has been declared a place of cultural, social and historical interest by the Canarian government, is a full-scale village built to illustrate the lifestyle of the Aborigens. Wax models and tableaux are used to show the activities of these people through all stages of life, from birth to death.

The islanders believed in a supreme god, and in demons as man's enemy. Mountain tops and high areas were used as places of worship and for making sacrifices.

A touch of reality is introduced by the use of real animals in the farming area. Goats, sheep and pigs formed the mainstay of the economy. Agriculture was restricted to crops, such as barley, wheat and beans, that could survive without irrigation. Special caves were made for grain storage (see Cenobio de Valerón, opposite).

The wheel remained unknown, and the tools and pottery shown here were all made by hand. Stone, wood and bone were the basic raw materials used in almost everything manufactured. Aborigen art consisted of simple geometric designs used to decorate pottery, and cave drawings.
ⓐ On the No 18 bus route between Playa del Inglés and Fataga
ⓣ 928 17 22 95 ⓛ 09.00–18.00 daily ⓘ Admission charge; restaurant facilities available

The mountainous interior of Gran Canaria

# Mountains of the interior

Choose a clear day for this day-long 168-km (104-mile) tour, which makes a circuit of all the island's high places. The highest village on the island and the highest peak are both included. Craggy mountain tops, famous rock monuments and forests of Canarian pine all present enduring images that contrast sharply with those left behind on the coast. On a fine day, there are views of Tenerife and Mount Teide from many points on the tour.

## THE ROUTE (see map on page 52)

The route starts and finishes in Playa del Inglés. Start off heading north along the Fataga Valley (see page 64) to San Bartolomé de Tirajana. From here, take the road to Tejeda and prepare for a winding route. The scenery changes dramatically on passing through a cutting known as Cruz Grande. Views previously restricted to the southern section of the island open up to encompass the central mountains.

Tiny Ayacata offers a chance for a break and refreshments at the El Montañón café. Stay on the road towards Tejeda but turn left, following the signs to Roque Bentaiga, when the junction is reached. The information centre lies beneath the parking area.

### Centro de Interpretación Roque Bentaiga

Roque Bentaiga is more than a significant landmark gracing the skyline: it has historical significance as a pre-Hispanic religious centre and is part of an archaeological park. Exhibits show how the entire ridge was inhabited by the Aborigens (see page 57) and that many of their cave dwellings are still in existence. The sacred nature of the rock is explained and some of the cave drawings exhibited. An information leaflet in English is available. ⓘ 928 66 61 89 (Tejeda tourist office) 🕒 11.00–17.00 daily

Return from the information centre back to the road and continue on to Tejeda, with its white cave houses clustered on a ridge. Turn left immediately after the village for Artenara. Take time along this cornice road, not just to enjoy the sweeping scenery but also because of the rough road surface.

More cave houses announce the approach of Artenara, which enjoys unequalled views from its perch on the mountainside.

**Artenara**

At 1,219 m (4,000 ft), Artenara is Gran Canaria's highest village. Well situated among fine scenery, it is another area of cave dwellings. There is a spacious viewpoint on the edge of town with seating for picnics.

Continue through Artenara on the road towards Teror, but prepare in time for the right turn towards Cruz de Tejeda. This junction coincides with a *mirador* (viewpoint) on the left, offering expansive views of Las Palmas. Cruz de Tejeda (see page 55) provides another opportunity to stretch the legs and perhaps shop for some local produce, such as *bienmasabe*, a honey and almond sauce, or cactus jam.

Leave Cruz de Tejeda by taking the small road signposted to Los Pechos. Watch out for the Degollada de Becerra information centre, which is well worth a stop.

*The view from the highest point on the island, Pozo de las Nieves*

**Degollada de Becerra Centro de Interpretación**
This centre, devoted to the geology, geomorphology, wildlife and traditions of the Nublo area, has a spectacular panoramic observation window with a chart designed to help visitors to identify the Roque Nublo and the surrounding rock formations.
928 21 92 29 11.00–17.00 daily

Continue ahead along this road, passing over the crossroads to follow the signs for **Pozo de las Nieves**. The road winds around the military establishment to end at the highest point on the island, 1,949 m (6,394 ft). Enjoy the unrivalled views before returning to the crossroads and turning left. Look out very shortly for the stopping place on the right for Roque Nublo (see below for a suggested walk). From here, the road leads to Ayacata, where a left turn leads back to Playa del Inglés.

**Roque Nublo walk**
This walk takes about 1 hour and 30 minutes to complete, and sensible footwear is essential. Start out from the car park, following the well-defined path. It quickly starts to climb beneath the slender El Fraile, to emerge on a saddle. Turn right here to continue climbing on to the table area (note your access point for the return), from where Roque Nublo is clear and obvious. Head towards the rock but prepare to return just before reaching the base of this natural monument, when it becomes more rocky and difficult underfoot. Return by the same route and, if you missed El Fraile on the way up, it is more clearly visible on the way back.

## TAKING A BREAK

Several small bars and restaurants in Artenara specialise in Canarian food, but it is advisable to check prices before ordering. (See also page 55.)

**Mesón la Silla ££** A moderately priced, popular cave restaurant (tends to attract coach parties). 928 56 61 08 Tues–Sun, closed Mon

# The Fataga Valley

Natural curiosities and landscapes are a major feature of this 120-km (75-mile) day-long tour, and there are plenty of opportunities for stretching your legs along the route. It starts by exploring the spectacular scenery of the Fataga Valley before heading back down towards sea level via Santa Lucía and on to Barranco de Guayadeque to look at the fascinating caves and cave restaurants.

## THE ROUTE (see map on page 52)

This somewhat circular tour starts and finishes in Playa del Inglés. Leave Playa del Inglés by heading due north towards San Bartolomé de Tirajana. The well-surfaced but narrow road leads in a steady ascent through a barren landscape. Static figures crouched in and around buildings of natural stone mark the site of **Mundo Aborigen** (see page 59). Shortly afterwards, where the road reaches a high point, there is a good viewpoint. Parking is on the left, but on a difficult corner that requires extreme care. Having reached the upper rim of the Fataga Valley, the route now descends into it.

### The Fataga Valley

The dramatic scenery of the Fataga Valley is one of the highlights of this tour. Rugged, towering mountains, set in a stark and barren countryside, decorated by nothing more than the cactus-like candlesticks of *Euphorbia canariensis*, give way to a green oasis as you progress up the valley. Nearby, palm-swamped Arteara is the location of an ancient Aborigen necropolis, **Necrópolis de Arteara** (see pages 57–8), and **Manolo's Camel Safari** (see page 74). Higher up the valley is another green oasis, this time at Fataga, where you can stop for a coffee or refreshments. Another area of green just beyond Fataga is the site of an old mill, now the attractive location of the restaurant **Molino de Agua de Fataga** (see page 66).

*The Fataga Valley*

On reaching San Bartolomé de Tirajana, take the road to Santa Lucía. Stop in the village for the Museo Castello de la Forteleza, the fort-like building on the main street.

**Museo Castillo de la Forteleza**

Natural sciences, archaeology, old weapons, folk and Aborigen artefacts rub shoulders in the 16 rooms of this well-presented museum. The castle-like building takes its name from the nearby Forteleza de Ansite (see page 66), but has no connection. The first exhibit is an old Canarian bedroom with a bed so high that steps are needed to climb in. Each room provides new surprises – stuffed birds, cases of mounted dragonflies, seashells imaginatively displayed in an old boat and even Roman amphorae (wine-storage jars). A restaurant and coffee bar are located in the rear gardens.

928 79 80 07 10.00–16.00 daily Admission charge

Soon after leaving the village, stay right for Agüimes (pronounced 'Awheemehz') and look for the two huge volcanic outcrops forming the Forteleza de Ansite.

**Forteleza de Ansite (Ansite Fort)**
Although this looks like a man-made fortress, it is an entirely natural volcanic rock. There is a viewpoint that gives an overview of the rock's history and its special significance to the Aborigens (see page 59).

From Agüimes, turn towards Ingenio but look immediately for the narrow street named La Orilla on the left, just as the houses come to an end. It is badly signposted and easily missed. This takes you right into Barranco de Guayadeque.

**Barranco de Guayadeque (Guayadeque Gorge)**
This ravine had strong connections with the Aborigens and has been declared a natural reserve. Many of the caves punctuating the walls of the ravine are still used as houses. Part-way up the valley, there is a whole cluster of cave houses which virtually constitute a village. Some of these, including a church, a bar and a restaurant, are at road level, while a steep path leads up to villagers' houses buried in the rock face. Near the end of the valley is a well-organised picnic site with tables. At the head of the valley lies the **Restaurant Tagoror** (see opposite), worth a visit if only for a drink before you return to Playa del Inglés.

## TAKING A BREAK

**Molino de Agua de Fataga £** Originally a watermill, this is now a hotel and restaurant serving full meals and snacks set among palm trees in pleasant rural surroundings. The reasonably priced menu offers grilled sirloin, pork chops and Canarian specialities such as the stewpot with chickpeas. Bring a swimming costume with you for a pre-lunch swim in the hotel pool. ⓐ Carretera de Fataga, just beyond Fataga ⓣ 928 17 20 89

Santa Lucía, one of the picturesque villages in the Fataga Valley

**Restaurant Tagoror £** Dine at moderate prices inside the cave or outside on the terrace. There is a choice of international fare and Canarian specialities. ⓐ Diputado Manuel Velázquez Cabrera 50, Jandia ⓣ 928 17 20 13 ⓒ 10.00–01.00 Mon–Thur, 10.00–02.00 Fri–Sun

# Zoos, gardens & the Wild West

Many of the island's most popular family attractions feature animals in some way or other. From crocodiles to performing parrots, the Wild West to giant cacti, there is plenty of variety on offer and amusement for all. The top attraction is Palmitos Park, but all the parks listed offer something unique.

**Jardín Botánico Canario (Canarian Botanic Garden)**
These extensive botanic gardens are devoted to the conservation and study of the Canarian flora. Not all the gardens are on the level – a large section ascends a steep embankment. There is a good information centre and a restaurant. Spring is the best time to visit, when the gardens show most colour.
ⓐ Carretera de Almatriche, Tafira Alta ⓣ 928 21 95 80 ⓦ www.jardin canario.org ◔ 09.00–18.00 daily, closed 1 Jan & Good Friday

**Palmitos Park**
Allow plenty of time to visit this subtropical oasis, home to some 1,500 tropical birds, representing 230 species. Not all are in cages: some are in their natural setting around lakes and many are free-flying. Birds apart, there is an orchid house full of exotic blooms and a huge aquarium, stocked with over 4,000 brilliantly coloured saltwater fish. The tropical butterfly house, claimed to be the first in Spain, presents a natural environment where butterflies can fly freely, although they spend a lot of time at rest, when they are much harder to spot. There is also an alligator section, a walk-in aviary and flamingo park, and a play area for the children.

From the entrance, a one-way route leads visitors around in a systematic manner, making sure that each particular attraction is seen, although it may be necessary to backtrack to the parrot show, which takes place every hour starting at 11.00. Some 15 parrots spend 25 minutes amusing and entertaining the audience with a whole range of skills and tricks.

A white-handed gibbon at Palmitos Park

There is a pizzeria and a café on-site, offering reasonably priced meals, drinks and snacks. Final call before leaving is the souvenir shop, where goods on sale have a distinct parrot flavour. After leaving the shop, keep an eye out for one more exhibit – the hard-to-spot hummingbirds.

Apart from all the attractions, the park is attractively laid out, with many different species of plants – all recently recatalogued – on view in the gardens. ⓐ Palmitos Park, Apartado 107, Maspalomas; bus No 45 runs a frequent service from Playa del Inglés and Maspalomas, with occasional No 70 buses from Puerto Rico and the Faro ⓣ 928 14 03 66/02 76 ⓕ 928 14 11 58 ⓦ www.palmitospark.es ⓛ 10.00–18.00 daily

## Parque de Cocodrilos (Crocodile Park)

Although the park boasts over 300 crocodiles, there is a much wider selection of birds and animals on show. Learn the difference between

crocodiles and alligators while wandering around the various enclosed pools. There is also a snake house, an aquarium and a reptile house to visit, and a parrot show to enjoy before reaching the animal section. Lively monkeys keep children entertained while the Bengal tigers pace relentlessly. Like Palmitos Park, the grounds are well planted with exotic plants, and the cactus garden is a bold feature.

ⓐ Villa de Agüimes ⓣ 928 78 47 25 ◷ 10.00–18.00 Sun–Fri, closed Sat

**Parque Norte**

This theme park is near the north coast of the island 3.5 km (2 miles) outside the town of Gáldar and not far from the two interesting Guanche sites of **Cueva Pintada** (see page 59) and the **Cenobio de Valerón** (see page 58). It is part garden, part zoo, and is intended to make for a family day out. The route through the park is about 1 km (⅔ mile) long and begins with a stroll through palm groves in which 80 different species from all over the world are grown. Another emblematic plant is the banana: an extensive collection of banana varieties illustrates how this plant is cultivated on the Canary Islands. Throughout the park there are also many colourful plants.

The zoo combines some familiar animals with many rare ones. Exotic birds include red-crowned cranes, toucans and parrots. Among the more unusual animals are cotton-topped tamarins from the Brazilian rainforest. There are also ducks and swans. A 'mini' subsection of the zoo has dwarf animal breeds including donkeys, pigs, goats, turtles and rabbits. When you need a break, there are two areas at the top and bottom of the park set aside for picnics.

ⓐ Carretera Sardina, Gáldar ⓣ 670 44 60 43 ⓦ www.parquenorte.es
◷ 10.00–17.30 daily

**Sioux City**

Built originally for the stage set of an American Western film back in the early 1970s, Sioux City has been preserved and developed as a Wild West theme park. Its dusty streets can be walked without fear and trepidation for most of the day, as you case the bank or check over the

Sheriff's Office, but be sure to find a shadowy corner and keep your head down at 13.30 and 16.30. This is when the show springs into life and the bullets really start to fly – not to mention the cows that stampede down the main street. Evocative country-and-western music, with shades of Clint Eastwood, adds atmosphere. It is all great fun for the children and, for a few dollars more, they too can be rigged out with hats and guns. Apart from the street entertainment, there is Miniature World for the children, and cowboy shows in the saloon at high noon and 15.00.

Special barbecue evenings are laid on for Friday evenings throughout the year. A free drink is included with the barbecue meal and country dancing supplements the Wild West show. Ask the tourist office for further information about this.

ⓐ Cañon del Aguila; bus No 29 to Sioux City leaves from the lighthouse in Playa del Inglés from 09.30 ⓣ 928 76 25 73 ◷ 10.00–17.00 Tues–Sun (Fri from 20.00 for barbecue night), closed Mon

*Sioux City re-creates a Wild West town*

# Water parks, trekking & go-karting

Theme parks are certainly a major form of holiday entertainment on Gran Canaria. Some of these demand active participation, and they include several aquatic parks, designed for fun in the water, as well as fairgrounds, camel safari parks and go-karting tracks where skilled experts can reach speeds of up to 80 km/h (50 mph). Here is a guide to the island's biggest and best.

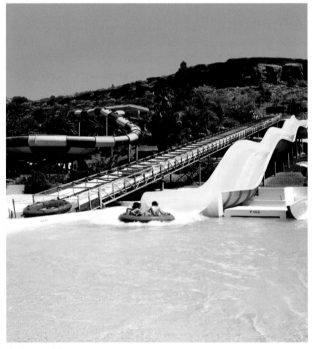

*The big slide at Aquapark*

## WATER PARKS

### Aqualand

This is the largest water park on Gran Canaria, featuring 29 different slides for thrill-seekers. The big slide is a straight race, with a whistle to start, but there are all sorts of slides, chutes, corkscrews and rides on a rubber ring. Announcements are made in advance when the wave machine comes into operation. A day spent here is fun for the whole family, with a small adventure playground (that carries an extra charge) for children. Sunbeds and shades are available, as well as drinks, snacks and meals, and all slides are supervised, with lifeguards on duty.

ⓐ Easily reached by Palmitos Park bus No 41 from Playa del Inglés or Maspalomas, and bus No 71 from Puerto Rico. Carretera Los Palmitos Park ⓣ 928 14 05 25 ⓦ www.aqualand.es ⓛ 10.00–17.00 daily ⓘ Ask the tourist office about discounted tickets

### Aquapark

Enough slides and chutes to keep families happy for hours, but smaller than Aqualand. It is not too conveniently located, at the very rear of the town.

ⓐ Motor Grande, Puerto Rico ⓣ 928 56 04 71 ⓛ 10.00–18.30 daily (summer); 10.00–17.30 daily (winter) ⓘ Ask the tourist office about discounted tickets

## CAMEL SAFARIS

Don't leave Gran Canaria without riding on a camel. Trekking across the famous Maspalomas sand dunes on a camel is one option but there are plenty of other opportunities. It's not unusual to find a few camels waiting outside any of the major attractions, but the properly organised events provide the best experience; ask the tourist office for details.

### La Baranda Camel Safari Park

Just a little further north than Manolo's (see page 74), there is a straightforward camel ride on offer here, with a restaurant on-site.

ⓐ The No 18 bus passes the door ⓣ 928 79 86 80/17 24 65 ⓛ 09.00–18.00 daily ⓘ Excursions: 20 min, €12; 30 min, €15 (prices at time of writing); children under 10 pay half price; a small charge is made to see the camels, watch the riders or use the facilities

**Manolo's Camel Safari**

Located in the village of Arteara in the Fataga Valley, the scenic surroundings here provide an ideal setting for a camel trek. Guests are welcomed with an aperitif before setting out through a palm oasis and along the valley to enjoy a simple meal out in the countryside.
ⓐ The No 18 bus passes by ⓣ 928 79 86 98

## HORSE TREKKING

**Canyon Horse Farm**

Also called The Black Horse, this ranch provides gentle treks for beginners as well as more challenging routes for advanced riders.
ⓐ From El Tablero (near Maspalomas) continue on to El Salobre
ⓣ 928 14 32 94

**Finca Hipisur Excursions**

Excursions of two to three hours around the southern countryside, for both beginners and experienced riders. Pick-up to and from your hotel, with drinks included in the price.
ⓐ Lomo Los Azures 31, Maspalomas ⓣ 679 86 70 57

## GO-KARTING

**Gran Karting Club**

Claiming the biggest track in the world – over 1,600 m (1 mile) long – this is a chance to test yourself at speeds reaching 80 km/h (50 mph). There is also a junior track, suitable for children from 12 to 16 years, and mini-motors are available for children over 5. Clubhouse facilities include drinks and snacks. Remember to check whether your insurance

is valid for this sport. Free transport here is provided if the group is large. (See also page 95.)

Tarajalillo 928 15 71 90 or 639 32 97 18 (for organised competitions)
11.00–22.00 daily (Apr–Sept); 10.00–21.00 daily (Oct–Mar)

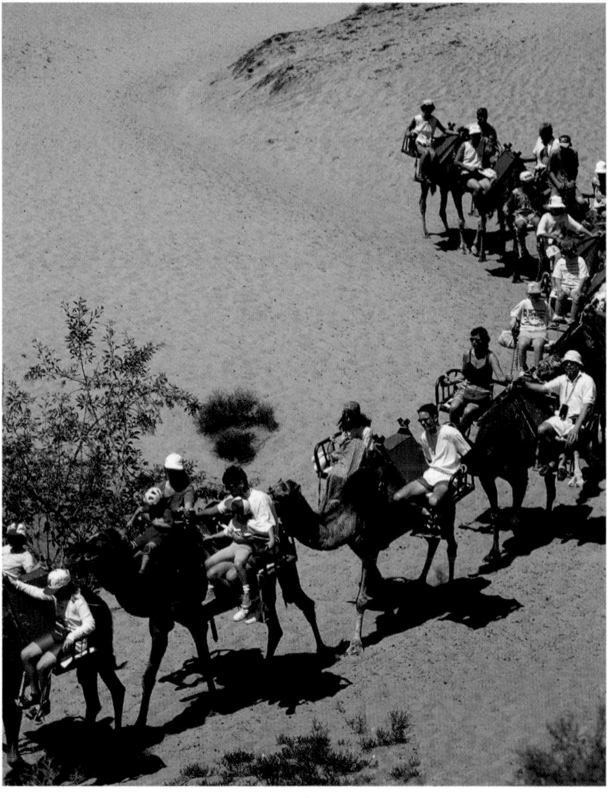

*Children will particularly enjoy camel rides*

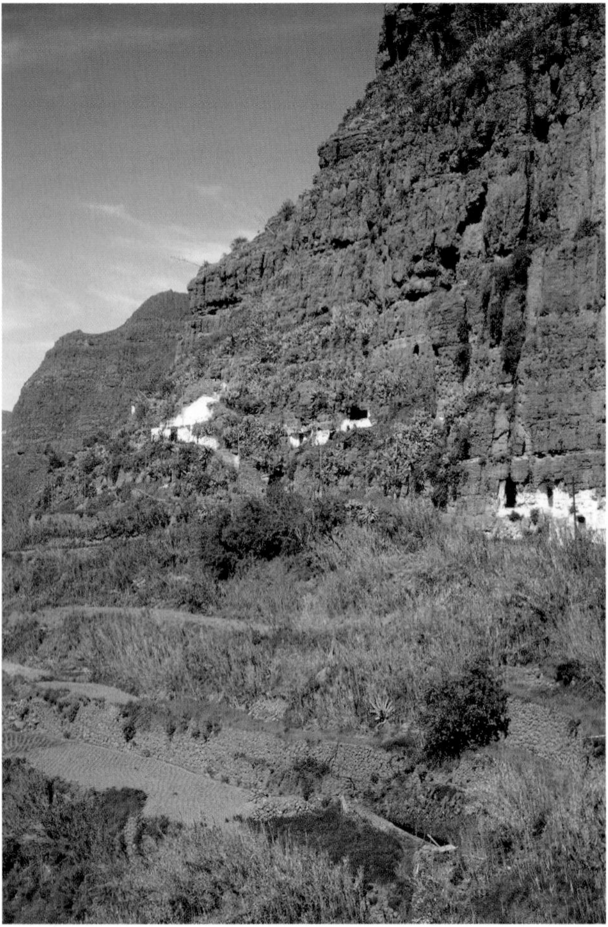

*The valley of Agaete is verdant*

# Northwestern Gran Canaria

The northwestern corner of the island is a perfect place to escape the commotion of the principal coastal resorts, and a chance to take in some of the fascinating culture of Gran Canaria. A new road links Las Palmas with Santa María de Guía (usually called simply Guía) and Gáldar, and this short tour, although an out-and-back route, is full of interest and opportunities to relax in a less crowded part of the island.

## THE ROUTE (see map on page 52)

Start at Playa del Inglés. Head up towards Las Palmas on the GC1, take the GC3, which branches off to the left at Jinamer and follow the signs to Gáldar, and then to Agaete/Guía. The 'motorway' to Agaete is well signposted, and this soon speeds you out along the northern coast of the island, with some attractive views of shingly beaches, where fishermen still cast their lines in Gran Canaria's time-honoured shore-fishing manner, next to rocky cliffs and crashing waves.

### Cenobio de Valerón (Convent of Valerón)

As you approach Guía, you have the opportunity to visit the Cenobio de Valerón, an amazing network of 200 caves, and one of the island's most important archaeological sites.

There is a tradition that this complex of caves was the abode of Guanche priestesses, who served the god Alcorac. Another story says that it was used to prepare young noblewomen for marriage, mainly by feeding them a high-calorie diet in readiness for motherhood. A more prosaic view, however, is that the caves were used as grain warehouses, and date from the Stone Age. (See also page 58.) 10.00–17.00 Tues–Sun, closed Mon

The road soon reaches Santa María de Guía; in fact, the road now bypasses the town, so you'll need to branch off. You can usually find somewhere to park along the main street.

**Santa María de Guía**

The old quarter of this ancient town is quite fascinating, a maze of narrow streets, many of them cobbled, that all lead (from a pronounced bend in the main road) up to the church.

The foundation of the town took place after the conquest of the island (1483), when Pedro de Vera distributed the lands between his soldiers and native noblemen. Among the first was Sancho de Vargas Machuca, who founded the hermitage, dedicated to 'Our Lady of Guía', around which the population grew. The church itself is a beautiful piece of 18th-century neoclassical work. The façade was built by locally born Luján Pérez, and it was on the organ here that French composer Camille Saint-Saëns gave the first performance of some of his works during a period when he stayed and worked in Guía.

Anyone feeling in need of a little refreshment in Guía will find the **Bar-Restaurante Tiscamanita**, on the main street, ideal. This may also be a place for a little souvenir shopping. If you want one of the elaborately carved knives for which the island is famous, you can get one at **Rafael Torres** on Calle 18 de Julio 48, but do remember not to carry it home as hand luggage.

By continuing down the main street, you soon reach a roundabout at the junction with the continuing motorway. Cross the roundabout and drive up towards Gáldar; you'll find room to park just before the first shops and bar-restaurants on the right as you enter the town.

**Gáldar**

This is the most historic of all Aborigen towns, and very proud to be so. It is shielded from the sea by the symmetrical cone of La Montana de Gáldar, and enjoys a pleasant climate. The town has an excellent covered market in the main street that is fascinating to wander around, but the *pièce de résistance* is the splendid Plaza de Santiago, a superb oasis of calm. One side of the square is occupied by the neoclassical church, which stands on the site of the palace of the former Aborigen kings. On another corner, you'll find the town hall, a magnificent building that contains in its courtyard the oldest dragon tree on the island (planted in 1718); the island's aboriginal people made use of its medicinal properties. The tourist office stands close by the monument to Tenesor Semidan, the last king of Gáldar.

Beyond Gáldar, the route continues easily to Agaete, winding pleasantly across the northwestern corner of the island to this prosperous little town, visited by only a small number of tourists.

### Agaete

This small town stands at the mouth of the verdant Agaete *barranco*, a gathering of attractive old buildings spreading out from the main square, one of the most agreeable spots on the whole island, and well worth the journey this far to experience. But beware: it is often very difficult to find a parking space, even early in the morning.

The church here, the Iglesia de la Concepción, has a fine 16th-century Flemish triptych that is displayed during the Bajada de la Rama, an ancient festivity celebrated both here and in the nearby harbour of Puerto de las Nieves (see Festivals & Events, page 104).

## TAKING A BREAK

**Casa Pepe £** Cheap, cheerful and good value. ⓐ Calle Alcalde Armas Galván 5, Agaete ⓣ 928 89 82 27 ◷ 12.00–18.00, 20.00–00.30 Thur–Tues, closed Wed

**Casa Romántica £** International and Spanish cuisine is available at a delightful eatery that makes a point of using fresh produce. ⓐ Lugar Culatilla, Agaete ⓣ 928 89 80 84

**Dedo de Dios ££** This seafood restaurant is popular with locals and tourists alike. For the best experience, lunch on grilled sardines, squid and paella at a sea-view window table. ⓐ Paseo de los Poetas, Puerto de las Nieves ⓣ 928 89 86 81 ◷ 12.00–22.00 Wed–Mon, closed Tues

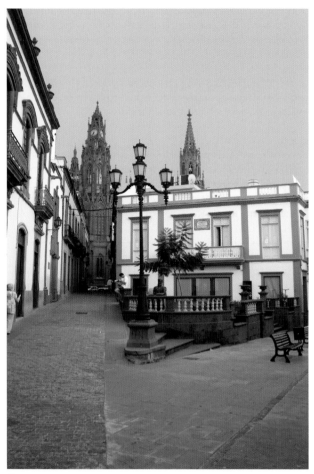

*Arucas, with its neo-Gothic church in the background (see page 84)*

# Northern Gran Canaria

Despite the sudden growth in popularity of the southern part of the island, the verdant and more fertile north remains the place to go to experience the best of traditional Canarian culture and society. Both of the island's pre-Hispanic kingdoms had their centres here (see page 57), and Las Palmas became one of the leading cities of the Spanish nation.

Inland from Las Palmas, the landscape is stunning, a rolling spread of volcanic mountains and villages where local architecture can still be found in abundance. It is all so much quieter and easy-going here; suddenly you find yourself back in time, where everything is taken at a more relaxed pace. Throughout this tour there are numerous places where you can stop off for a drink or something to eat; every village has its bar-restaurants, so finding somewhere to take a break is easy.

## THE ROUTE (see map on page 52)

From Playa del Inglés, take the GC1 north until the GC3 branches off to the left to Tafira. Follow the Tafira signs until the GC3 finishes and changes into the C811, going from Tafira Baja to Tafira Alta.

From Las Palmas, take the GC3 from Tamaraceite to where it joins the C811 to Tafira Baja. Between the two villages, look out for the signposted turning to the Jardín Botánico Canario. This may well be a convenient time for you to visit this large botanic garden (see page 68).

### Santa Brígida

The route now winds onwards and upwards to the prosperous villa town of Santa Brígida, which has become a well-to-do suburb of Las Palmas, possessing rather less of the true Spanish atmosphere than you might expect on first impressions. Its tree-lined streets and villages with large gardens actually owe their origins to the early British settlers, who came here to begin winemaking and, later, banana-producing businesses.

### Vega de San Mateo

From Santa Brígida, the route continues to prosperous Vega de San Mateo, better known by its shortened name of San Mateo. The town stands among the foothills of the Tejeda crater. Cultivation terraces here produce substantial crops of fruit and vegetables, including almonds, chestnuts and figs. There is a popular weekend morning market here, so be warned that it becomes busy. However, if you want to take time out to wander round the market, it offers a good selection of fresh fruit and vegetables, home-grown herbs and local cheeses and wines. Perhaps not surprisingly, the town church is dedicated to the patron saint of farmers and cattle breeders.

Beyond San Mateo, you head up into the Parque Rural del Nublo, through a landscape so stunning that it is difficult not to keep stopping to admire and photograph your surroundings. Stay on the main road, ignoring diversions, and eventually you arrive at the Cruz de Tejeda, which marks the notional centre of the island, at nearly 1,490 m (4,890 ft) (see page 55). The square in which it is set has seen better days, but it is certainly worth trying the lunchtime restaurant here for the exceptional terrace views, which embrace Roques Nublo and Bentaiga.

### Tejeda

For many visitors, the Cruz de Tejeda marks the turning-back point in their visit. However, this optional extension zigzags downwards into a peaceful landscape ignored by most and dotted with isolated groups of white houses with pantiled roofs. The objective of this route (which will see you later return to the Cruz) is to visit the peaceful and very attractive mountain village of Tejeda. A serpentine road descends from the Cruz to this village, which each year celebrates the Festival of the Almond Blossom, *Almendra en Flor*. Here, you can get refreshments at any of a number of small bar-restaurants – at the **Cueva de la Tea** and the **Terraza Gayfa**, for example. It is very tempting to stay in this peaceful spot for quite a while, which is a remarkable contrast if your base is somewhere like Playa del Inglés or Puerto Rico.

Go back up to the Cruz, and down the road on the other side, but keep an eye open for the turning to Valleseco. On the way, and in Valleseco itself, opportunities present themselves to stop and take pictures, especially at the **Mirador de Zamora**, where the large restaurant does a lively trade.

### Firgas

Beyond the restaurant, continue to Firgas, the 'capital' of the smallest municipality on Gran Canaria, and famed throughout the islands for its natural spring water, although it also produces bananas, watercress and yams. The main road bypasses Firgas, so if you want to spend some time there, you will have to divert; the signposting is obvious.

*The mountainous north of the island*

**Arucas**

After that, head for the town of Arucas. Its most remarkable feature is the sharply pointed, neo-Gothic church of San Juan Bautista, so magnificently built it resembles a cathedral. Started in 1909, it was not completed until 1977, although it looks considerably older.

Arucas used to be known as 'the town of flowers', and it has fine subtropical gardens in the main park. Outside the town, virtually all the greenery is composed of banana plantations. Northeast of the town rises the volcanic cone of Montaña de Arucas, where the last renowned aboriginal freedom fighter, Doramas, was killed in 1481. A brief visit will reward you with fine views of La Isleta and the bay of Las Palmas.

After leaving Arucas, you gradually work your way towards Las Palmas, via Tamaraceite. The way through is adequately signposted, and generally easy enough to follow.

## TAKING A BREAK

Santa Brígida is renowned for its restaurants:

**Cafetería Churrería Mall £** Ideal for a late (or second) breakfast.
ⓐ Near the post office

**Casa Martel ££** This old-fashioned restaurant has an excellent wine cellar. ⓣ 928 64 12 83 ⓛ 12.00–17.00 daily

**Los Gerianos ££** An inexpensive place serving grilled and roast pork and local red wine. ⓣ 928 35 55 77

**Les Grutes de Artiles £££** A classy (and expensive) choice.
ⓐ Las Meleguines ⓣ 928 64 05 75

◗ *Examples of local pottery*

# LIFESTYLE

## Island life

# Food & drink

Eating out on Gran Canaria can be relatively cheap, especially in typical Canarian restaurants, although these tend to be thin on the ground in more popular tourist areas such as Playa del Inglés, where international menus predominate. For a real Canarian experience, it is much better to find a restaurant frequented by the locals or head out to inland villages. Local food is delicious and certainly not to be avoided. Many traditional dishes originate from earlier times when there was a limited variety of ingredients. Later inhabitants introduced new ideas and a wider range of fruit and vegetables, to develop what has become a very wholesome and delicious cuisine.

## EATING OUT

The local papers have advertisements and lists of restaurants, while in the streets, people hand out flyers touting for custom that will give you an idea of what to expect.

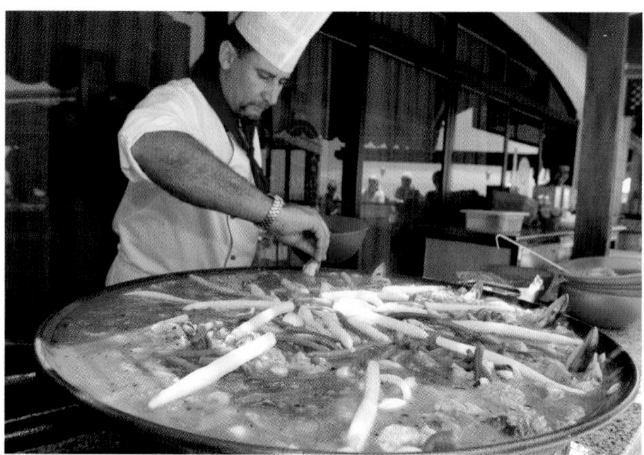

*A chef making paella*

A good source of information for finding the best places to eat is the holiday company representative at your hotel; he or she will have first-hand reports from other clients. Whatever your tastes, Gran Canaria can provide for them. There is traditional British – be it full English breakfast, Sunday roast with Yorkshire puddings, bangers and mash, or fish and chips. There is even Kentucky Fried Chicken, Pizza Hut and McDonald's, if you must.

European and Asian restaurants abound, top of the list being Spanish, followed by Chinese, Indian, Italian, German, French, Scandinavian, Thai, Korean and Mexican. Popular with the Canarians are Venezuelan restaurants – try their freshly prepared *arepas*, savoury South American pancakes.

Every Canarian town and village has a bar or two and practically all will be able to produce food, so one never needs to go hungry.

## LOCAL FOOD

Once a staple food of the pre-Hispanic population, *gofio*, toasted maize or wheat, ground into flour, is still a feature in many recipes. It was once made into bread, but is now used as a thickener or made into dumplings. Canarian soups are more like stews and are virtually a meal

### TAPAS

An interesting way to sample a variety of Canarian dishes is to seek out a tapas bar – the Spaniards' own version of a fast-food outlet. There are many such bars in Las Palmas and in local communities, but you will be hard pressed to find one in tourist areas. Tapas are served in small portions (*tapa* means 'lid' or 'small dish') but if something more substantial is required, ask for a medium size – *medio ración* – or a large portion to share between two – a *ración* (pronounced 'rassion'). The problem here is knowing what to ask for, so go armed with the names of some dishes or be brave and choose at random from the display on the counter.

*Treat yourself to a traditional meal*

in themselves, so choose carefully if you are aiming for three courses. Fresh vegetables are plentiful, as is fish (salted and fresh), which is usually boiled, fried or grilled and served with a *mojo* (pronounced 'moho') sauce. Meats, such as goat, rabbit and pork, are found locally, but other meat – steak, for example – is imported especially for tourists. Cheese, mostly made from goat's milk, is an important accompaniment to a meal, and the Canaries boast many varieties – mild *queso flor*, 'flower cheese', from Guía, is a popular choice.

## WINE

A small quantity of wine is still produced near Las Palmas, but the large selection of wine in the shops is imported from mainland Spain. Two reasonably priced Riojas are Campo Vieja and Siglo, but there is a huge selection to sample.

Gran Canaria and the other islands have cheaper prices for alcoholic drinks than mainland Spain and the rest of the EU. It is usually wise to ask specifically for a brand name, as the cheaper Spanish alternatives may not be to your liking.

There is an incredible selection of spirits, but be warned that measures are triple or quadruple the size of British measures. The *ron* (rum) is a white spirit made on Gran Canaria from sugar cane. It is consumed by the locals, who often drink it with coffee. *Ron miel*, a dark liqueur, is a mixture of rum and honey – warming on a cool evening. Or you could try the unique, sweet flavour of the banana liqueur, *cobana*. This makes an unusual souvenir as it is sold in a bottle shaped like a bunch of bananas.

International makes of canned beers are now widely available, such as Heineken, Worthington and even Guinness®. The local lager, Dorada, comes on tap and in cans and is quite thirst-quenching. *Sangría*, a mixed drink served in a big glass jug with lots of fruit and ice, is often chosen by tourists. Beware – this attractive-looking drink can be very alcoholic. More innocuous is *zumo*, which is freshly squeezed fruit juice. Try a mixture of *naranja* (orange), *limón* (lemon) and *melocotón* (peach).

# Menu decoder

**SNACKS/SIDE ORDERS, TAPAS**

**Aceitunas en mojo** Olives in hot sauce

**Almogrote** Cheese paste spread

**Bocadillo** Filled roll

**Champiñones al ajillo** Mushrooms sautéed with garlic

**Chipirones** Small squid

**Ensalada** Salad

**Gambas ajillo** Garlic prawns

**Papas arrugadas** Small jacket potatoes boiled in very salty water served with a *mojo picante* (hot chilli sauce) or *mojo verde* (herb and garlic sauce)

**Perrito caliente** Hot dog

**Queso** Cheese

**Tapas** Snacks

**STARTERS**

**Potaje** Thick vegetable soup – may contain added meat

**Potaje de berros** Watercress soup

**MAIN COURSES**

**Cabrito** Kid (goat)

**Caldo de escado** Fish, maize-meal stew and vegetables

**Conejo al salmorejo** Rabbit in hot chilli sauce

**Garbanzas** Chickpea stew with meat

**Lomo** Slices of pork

**Pata de cerdo** Roast leg of pork

**Pechuga empanada** Breaded chicken breast or chicken breast in batter

**Puchero** Meat and vegetable stew

**Ranchos** Noodles, beef and chickpeas

**Ropa vieja** Chickpeas, vegetables and potatoes (although meat can be added)

**Sancocho** Salted fish (often *cherne*, a kind of sea bass) with potatoes and sweet potatoes

**DESSERTS**

**Arroz con leche** Cold rice pudding

**Bienmesabe** A mix of honey and almonds (delicious poured over ice cream)

**Flan** Crême caramel

**Fruta del tiempo** Fresh fruit in season

**Helado** Ice cream

**Truchas** Turnovers filled with pumpkin jam

**DRINKS**

**Agua mineral** Mineral water – may be *con gas/ sin gas*, fizzy/still

**Batido** Milkshake

**Bitter kas** Similar to Campari but non-alcoholic

**Café** Coffee – served *con leche* (with milk), as a *cortado* (small white coffee), *descafeinado*, (decaffeinated) or *solo* (black)

**Cerveza** Beer

**Cocktail Atlántico** Rum, dry gin, banana liqueur, blue curaçao, pineapple nectar

**Cocktail Canario** Rum, banana cream liqueur, orange juice, Cointreau, a drop of grenadine

**Guindilla** Rum-based cherry liqueur

**Leche** Milk

**Limonada** Lemonade

**Mora** Blackberry liqueur

**Naranja** Orange

**Ron** Local rum

**Ron miel** Rum with honey, a local speciality

**Sangría** Mix of red wine, spirits and fruit juices; can be made with champagne on request

**Té** Tea

**Vino** Wine – comes as *blanco*, which is white; *rosado*, which is rosé; or *tinto*, which is red

**Zumo** Juice

# Shopping

Although part of the EU, Gran Canaria has special duty-free status, so it is treated as a non-EU territory for allowances. This means that, tempting as it is to spend and spend on the duty-free goods that dominate many of the shopping centres, there is a limit to the value of goods (and separate allowance for tobacco and alcohol) that can be

*The market at Puerto de Mogán*

brought back to the UK without attracting import tax. These allowances vary, so ask for information on the latest duty-free allowances.

## BARGAINING

Expect to bargain in markets and at many of the duty-free shops, and note that marked prices are usually highly inflated.

A simple technique for bargaining is to show an interest in the goods and then start to walk away. The price drops instantly, so show renewed interest, and then turn away again. Another price reduction will be offered. This is the starting point for making an offer. It is not advisable to spend serious money without first checking out a few suppliers.

## SOUVENIRS

If you are looking for souvenirs unique to the island, you might consider:

- Baskets made from woven banana leaves or rushes, such as might be seen in Teror.
- A knife with a handle inlaid with bone and horn (take this home in a suitcase, not in hand luggage, or you risk having it confiscated as an offensive weapon).
- Lace, especially from Ingenio, Agüimes and Tirjana. Lace and linen tablecloths are also freely available in the markets. These are often imported but they can still be good value. Goods carrying a FEDAC label guarantee that the product has been made by craftspeople.
- *Bienmesabe* (a honey and almond sauce), and melon, almond and peach liqueurs.

## AIRPORT SHOPPING

The departure lounge has an extensive shopping mall, complete with Burger King, sandwich bars, restaurants, cafés and play areas for children. Enjoy last-minute duty-free shopping for clothing (from **Tie Rack**, **Leather House** and **American World**), for Canarian specialities and souvenirs, and for flowers. Goods in the airport are no cheaper than those sold in the shops on Gran Canaria, since the whole island is a duty-free area.

# Children

There is plenty to entertain children on Gran Canaria. Mountains of sand surround the southern coastal resorts and the deep dunes at Maspalomas provide endless hours of fun. Off the beach, there are enough activities to keep children happily occupied.

## FUN WITH THE ANIMALS

Children are fascinated by animals and there are plenty of zoos and theme parks to visit. Parque de Cocodrilos, with more than 300

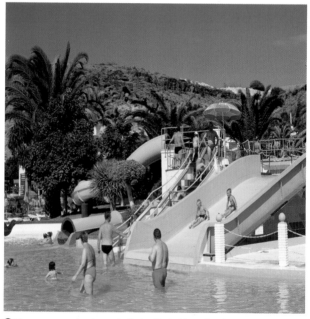

*There are several water parks that will provide endless fun*

crocodiles, as well as many other animals and shows, is a fantastic day out (see pages 69–70).

Sioux City offers Wild West shows and offers many attractions for children. Increasing the number of animals is at the heart of the scheme and the intention is to import 15 mini-horses, four mini-donkeys and 12 American buffalo. There will also be a Ferris wheel. Birthday parties can be arranged for children at Sioux City at fairly short notice (see pages 70–71 for further details). Camel rides are also available at many places on the island (see pages 73–4).

## MINI-GOLF

Plenty of mini-golf facilities are open late, so it is not necessary to surrender prime beach time. The first of two in Playa del Inglés, **Taidia Mini-Golf**, has a pool table and drinks (Ⓐ Avenida de Tirajana, behind Supermercado Cadena Maraga Ⓛ 10.00–00.30 daily ⓘ Small charge). Another is **San Valentine Park** (Ⓐ Avenida Sargentos Provisionales 26 Ⓣ 928 76 10 77 Ⓛ 09.00–23.00 daily ⓘ Small charge).

## THE MINI-TRAIN

The Mini-Train, or Choo-Choo train, tours the streets of Playa del Inglés. Children and families ride in open but shaded carriages in a long snake behind the engine. It must be joined at Avenida Italia 12.

## SWIMMING, DIVING & GO-KARTING

There is a pleasant swimming pool behind the beach in Puerto Rico, which caters well for children, not to mention the big water parks such as Aqualand (see page 73). Gran Karting Club (see pages 74–5) has the largest go-karting track in Spain, but also caters for children. Apart from the junior track, suitable for children between the ages of 12 and 16, there are mini-motors for children over 5 to try out. Mini-bikes are a more recent addition to the entertainment, and are suitable for those over the age of 10. Or try a thrilling trip to the bottom of the sea on the *Yellow Submarine* in Puerto de Mogán (see page 43).

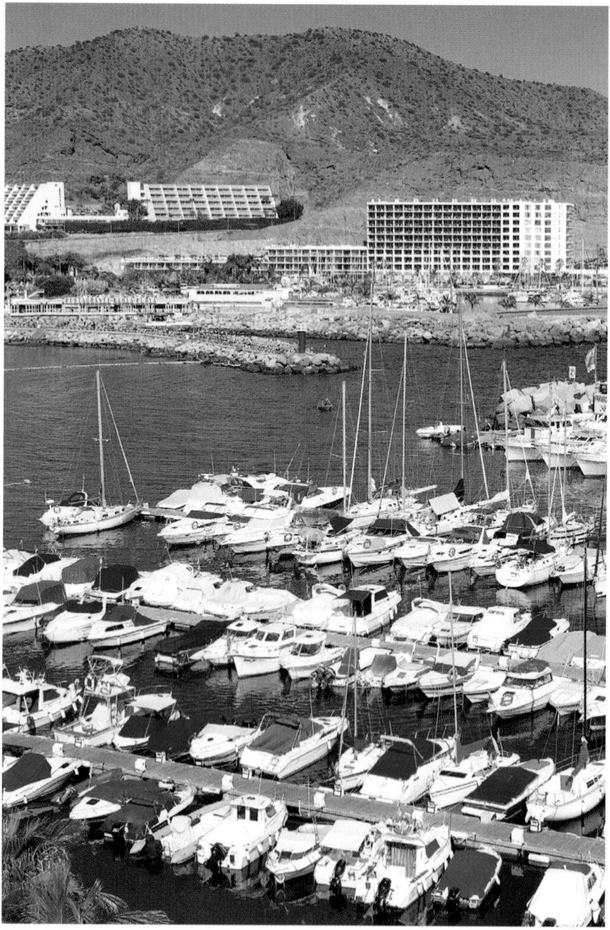

*Puerto Rico harbour is a popular base for cruises*

# Sports & activities

Good sea temperatures throughout the year are an advantage for sea-sport enthusiasts on Gran Canaria. This makes conditions for watersports ideal around the shores of the island, which hosts more than its share of international events.

September is the warmest month, when sea temperatures reach an average of 23.3°C (74°F), while winter temperatures remain around 19°C (67°F), just dipping below in March, although nights can be chilly. Puerto Rico is one of the island's most important centres for water activities, while golf courses, horse riding and bike tours are also on offer throughout the island.

## CRUISING

Cruising is perhaps a grand term, but there are one or two boats offering sea trips with entertainment, lunch and opportunities for swimming.

### Dolphin search trip

The *Spirit of the Sea*, a glass-bottom catamaran based in Puerto Rico, offers two-hour trips to look for dolphins and whales.
t 928 56 22 29 w www.dolphin-whale.com e spirit@dolphin-whale.com Trips leave daily at 10.00, 12.30 & 15.00

### *Supercat*

*Supercat* is claimed to be the world's largest catamaran and offers daytime and evening cruises that can be booked through holiday reps, hotels or directly.
a Puerto Rico harbour t 928 15 02 48

### *Timanfaya*

*Timanfaya* is another sailing ship offering excursions along the southwest coast.
a Out of Puerto Rico harbour; a special passenger bus runs from Playa del Ingés, with various pick-up points along the way t 928 26 82 80

## GOLF

**Anfi Tauro Golf** An 18-hole championship course. ⓐ Near Mogán by the Time-Share complex ⓣ 928 12 88 40/41 ⓦ www.anfi.com

**Campo de Golf** Located adjacent to the famous sand dunes in Maspalomas, this 18-hole, par-73 course is long, at 6,216 m (6,800 yds). Other facilities include a driving range, putting green, and trolley and club hire. Apart from a clubhouse, there is a restaurant and snack service. ⓐ Avenida Neckerman, Maspalomas ⓣ 928 76 25 81 ⓕ 928 76 82 45 ⓦ www.maspalomasgolf.net ❗ Special rates are offered to juniors under the age of 18

*Campo de Golf*

**Cortijo Club de Campo** This new 18-hole course with lakes and palm trees is 6 km (4 miles) from Las Palmas and ten minutes north of the airport. ⓐ Autopista del Sur GC1, Km 6.4, 35218 Telde ⓣ 928 71 11 11 ⓕ 928 71 49 05 ⓦ www.elcortijo.es

**Meloneras Golf** An 18-hole course located in Meloneras Bay in the south of the island. ⓣ 928 14 53 09

**Las Palmeras Golf** An 18-hole course close to the centre of Las Palmas with views of Las Canteras beach. ⓐ Avenida Dr Alfonso Chiscano Díaz, Las Palmas ⓣ 928 22 23 33 ⓦ www.laspalmerasgolf.es

**Real Club de Golf de Las Palmas** Founded originally in Las Palmas in 1891, this golf club was relocated to Bandama in 1956. The 18-hole, par-71 course, designed by Mackenzie Ross, is a fairly testing 5,679 m (6,213 yds) long. Facilities include a good clubhouse and restaurant, practice tees, two putting greens and a sports shop. ⓐ Santa Brígida, 14 km (nearly 9 miles) from Las Palmas, adjacent to the Bandama Crater ⓣ 928 35 01 04 ⓦ www.realclubdegolfdelaspalmas.com ⓛ Tee-time 08.00–12.50 Mon–Fri, members only at weekends

**Salobre Golf** An 18-hole course with clubhouse, café and restaurant. ⓐ Situated in the mountains behind Pasito Blanco off the GC1, 53 km (33 miles) south of Maspalomas ⓣ 928 01 01 03 ⓕ 928 01 01 04 ⓦ www.salobregolfresort.com

## HORSE RIDING

**Canyon Horse Farm** (see page 74).

**Finca Hipisur Excursions** (see page 74).

## QUAD-BIKE SAFARIS & BIKE TOURS

For the adventurous, there is always the possibility of going on a mountain-bike tour, or a quad-bike safari, driving along dry river beds and mountain paths. For those who prefer a more leisurely pace, a good option is a bicycle tour, on paved roads, to places of beauty.

**Free Motion Tours** ⓣ 928 77 74 79 ⓕ 928 77 52 99 ⓦ www.free-motion.net ⓔ info@free-motion.net

## SAILING & WINDSURFING SCHOOLS

There are several schools on the island offering sailing and windsurfing tuition for all levels.

**Real Club Victoria** Offers windsurfing lessons for children and adults, and Optimist sailing for children 8–14. ⓐ Paseo de las Canteras 4, Las Palmas ⓣ 928 46 06 30 (club), 928 46 25 14/46 24 72 (school)

## SCUBA DIVING

Classes for beginners are offered by a number of schools on the island, and there are plenty of opportunities for diving for the more experienced:

**Aquanauts Dive Centre** ⓐ On the beachfront at Puerto Rico ⓣ 928 73 61 96 ⓦ www.aquanauts-divecenter.com

**Calypso Divers** Diving excursions for all levels. English spoken, and all equipment provided. ⓐ Hotel Mirador, Maspalomas, Sonneland ⓣ/ⓕ 928 56 61 69 ⓦ www.divingcalypso.net

**Centro Náutico de Buceo** Equipment for 40 divers. ⓐ Hotel IFA Interclub Atlantic, San Agustín ⓣ 620 94 77 53 ⓛ 09.00–18.00 daily

**PADI Diving School/Nordic Divers** ⓐ Based at the Aeroclub ⓣ 660 29 18 91 ⓦ www.lgdiving.com

**Top Diving** Provides organised group expeditions. ⓐ Puerto Rico ⓣ 928 56 06 09 ⓛ Departures at 10.00 and 14.00 daily

## SEA FISHING

Offshore fishing is especially good around the island, with the opportunity to fish for tuna, white and blue swordfish and shark.

**Sea fishing** ⓐ Leaving from Puerto Rico ⓣ/ⓕ 928 56 55 21 (ask for Antonio); alternatively 659 69 24 25 (ask for Roberto)

## SURFING

This is a year-round activity on Gran Canaria, but the best waves are generally experienced between September and March. The north, near Gáldar, offers the most challenging conditions, with waves as high as 5 m (16 ft) at times. When the wind is in the east, a good place for surfing is in the Bay of Pozo Izquierdo in the southeast of the island. In the south, the beach just west of the lighthouse in Maspalomas and Arguineguin provides a good spot.

## TENNIS & SQUASH

**Tenis Holycan** ⓐ Calle Holanda, Maspalomas ⓣ 928 76 77 46

## WALKING

Some 308 km (186 miles) of footpaths have already been restored on the island for walkers to enjoy, and work continues to repair and rebuild more of these. All paths are in the upland areas towards the centre and in the north of Gran Canaria. Unfortunately, information about the paths has not managed to keep up with the pace of restoration. The best walking book, available at bookshops on the island, is *Landscapes of Gran Canaria*, published by Sunflower Books, and this is revised regularly, or you can contact the Gran Canaria Tourist Board. ⓣ 928 21 96 00 ⓦ www.grancanaria.com

## WATERSKIING & JET-SKIING

There are plenty of opportunities for waterskiing and jet-skiing in all the main southern resorts.

## WINDSURFING

There are two particular places in the north of the island, near Gáldar and at Puerto de las Nieves, which are highly favoured by expert windsurfers, but generally the southernmost part of the island provides conditions more suitable for beginners and improvers.

Equipment can be hired at many beaches in the south, but there are two windsurfing schools that offer tuition to both beginners and improvers:

**Club Mistral Canarias** ⓐ Playa de Tarajalillo 5 ⓣ 928 15 71 58 ⓛ 09.30–17.30 daily

**Puerto Rico Sailing School** ⓐ Puerto Rico, Puerto Escala ⓣ 928 56 52 92/609 58 59 33 ⓛ Mon–Sat (Sept–July), closed Sun

# Festivals & events

There is nothing the Canarians enjoy more than a good fiesta. Any significant event is celebrated and turned into a street party. Some fiestas have deep religious significance but most are a lively mixture of fun and exuberance.

Every village celebrates the feast day of its own patron saint, with local and national days to celebrate as well. **Carnaval**, the greatest and most colourful of them all, takes place in February or March, to coincide with the start of Lent. Celebrations across the island culminate in a grand fancy-dress party and a masked parade that goes on for hours.

In Playa del Inglés, Carnaval takes over the Yumbo Centre for about two weeks and there are many local events organised, including in the Parque Santa Catalina or the Plaza Santa Ana in Las Palmas. The curtain finally descends with a solemn procession for the Burial of the Sardine.

Other important celebrations include:

- The Feast of the Three Kings on 6 January; this marks the Canarian Christmas and is widely celebrated on the island.
- The Almond Blossom Festival, around late February in Valsequillo and Tejeda. Lots of music and dancing, food and drink.
- May Day is a holiday which is usually celebrated by parades, although they often take place on the first Sunday in May.
- Corpus Christi, 17 June, is special in Las Palmas. The streets around the cathedral are decorated with flowers, sand and pebbles made into patterns and pictures.
- Teror observes its own special day, 8 September, with the most important religious celebration on the island.

### CANARIAN WRESTLING

This unusual sport is very popular on Gran Canaria. Traditionally, the wrestling takes place in a sand-covered arena and involves a team of 12 people. The loser is the one who touches the ground with any part of the body (apart from the feet) during a hold.

## MUSIC FESTIVAL ATLANTA

Every year, during the month of March, a two-day music festival, with acts from Spain, Britain and other countries, is held on the beach in Playa del Inglés. The date varies, so check with the tourist office.

## SAN FERNANDO FAIR

This lively affair takes place for a week in May each year, with all the usual fun of the fair, plenty of sideshows and entertainment for all ages.

## WHAT'S ON WHEN

Gran Canaria has an amazing wealth of festivals and celebrations. For festival information: t 928 77 15 50 w www.grancanaria.com

### January

- Feast of the Three Kings (see opposite).

### February

- Almond Blossom Festival (see opposite).
- Carnaval (see opposite): a week of celebrations with processions, street bands and all-night street parties.

### March

- Arguineguin: Feast Day of Santa Agueda.

### April

- Fiesta de los Aborigenes: commemorates the defeat of the indigenous people. Held on 29 April in Las Palmas; lots of music and dancing.

### May

- Apricot Festival in Fataga.

### June

- Corpus Christi (see opposite) in Las Palmas and Arucas. Carpets of flowers, sawdust and sand cover the route of a procession.

**July**

- Fiestas del Carmen: 16 July. Celebrated in traditional fishing villages.
- Romería al Señor de los Caballeros: held in Gáldar on 25 July. Goes on for about 20 days, with Canarian music, dancing and wrestling.

**August**

- Bajada de la Rama: Agaete's fiesta, 4 August. An aboriginal festival, from pre-Hispanic days – the island's most popular festival.

**September**

- Feast of Our Lady of the Pine: the island's patron saint, on 8 September in Teror. A great and moving pilgrimage – many walk to Teror through the night to render homage, with singing and dancing.
- Fiesta del Charco: in San Nicolás de Tolentino on 10 September. A traditional immersion in water that is re-enacted each year.

**October**

- Fiestas de Nuestra Señora del Rosario: on 5 October in Agüimes, with traditional stick fighting, Canarian wrestling and flower battles.
- La Naval: on 6 October in Las Palmas. Commemorates the successful repulse of Sir Francis Drake from the islands in 1595.

**November**

- Rancho de Ánimas: peculiar to Teror – between November and January. Groups of mainly elderly men roam the streets singing.

**December**

- Feast Day of Santa Lucía: 13 December.
- Fiesta de los Labradores: Santa Lucía, on 20 December. Everyone celebrates by dressing in peasant costume.

*An old farmhouse near Firgas*

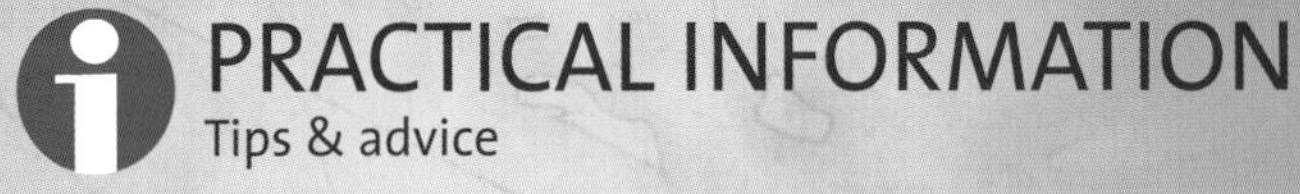

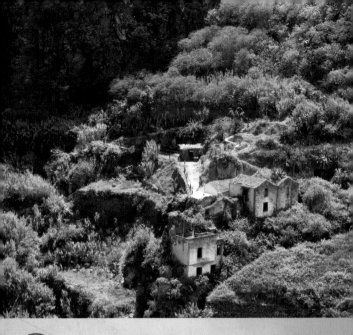

# PRACTICAL INFORMATION

## Tips & advice

# Accommodation

The accommodation ratings in this book are as follows:
**£** up to €90 **££** €90–€150 **£££** over €150

All prices are per double room per night in high season and are based on two people sharing, without breakfast.

**Fonda de la Tea £** A restored 19th-century guesthouse with 11 rooms giving mountain views over the magnificent landscapes of inland Gran Canaria. ⓐ Ezequiel Sánchez 22, Tejeda ⓣ 928 66 64 22 ⓦ www.hotelfondadelatea.com

**Magnolias Natura £** Naturist complex of self-contained bungalows arranged around a large pool. No children under 12 allowed. ⓐ Avenida Touroperador Tjaereborg, Campo Internacional, Maspalomas ⓣ 928 77 01 22 ⓦ www.canariasnatura.com

**Princesa Guayarmina £** A spa hotel in a lush setting. Health treatments on offer include acupuncture and massage. ⓐ Los Berrazales, Agaete ⓣ 928 89 80 09

**Las Calas ££** A homely farmhouse off the Las Palmas–Cruz de Tejeda road through the middle of the island. Comfortable and informal. ⓐ El Arenal, 38 La Lechuza, Vega de San Mateo ⓣ 928 66 14 36 ⓦ www.hotelrurallascalas.com

**Casa de Los Camellos ££** Charming hotel of 12 double rooms grouped around two patios. Restaurant. ⓐ Progreso 12, Agüimes ⓣ 928 78 50 03 ⓦ www.hecansa.com

**Escuela Santa Brígida ££** Well-equipped yet reasonably priced hotel which is handily located for getting into Las Palmas. ⓐ Real de Coello 2, Santa Brígida ⓣ 928 35 55 11 ⓦ www.hecansa.com

**Eugenia Victoria ££** Good value for the high level of services and comfort provided. Free shuttle bus to the beach. ⓐ Avenida de Gran Canaria 26, Playa del Inglés ⓣ 928 76 25 00 ⓦ www.bullhotels.com

**Finca Las Longueras ££** Known as the 'Red House', this large colonial house stands in a plantation of subtropical fruit trees. ⓐ Valle de Agaete, Agaete ⓣ 928 89 81 45 ⓦ www.laslongueras.com

**La Hacienda del Molino ££** A restaurant, museum and hotel all rolled into one, in a former *gofio* (corn flour) mill. ⓐ Calle Los Naranjos 2, Tunte, San Bartolomé de Tirajana ⓣ 928 12 73 44 ⓦ www.lahaciendadelmolino.com

**Maipez Hotel Rural ££** Peaceful location in the north of the island. ⓐ Carretera La Calzada 104, Calzada ⓣ 928 28 72 72 ⓦ www.maipez.com

**Reina Isabel ££** The best mid-price option if you want to stay in the capital. ⓐ Alfredo L Jones 40, Las Palmas ⓣ 928 26 01 00 ⓦ www.bullhotels.com

**Gloria Palace Amadores £££** A hotel which rises impressively above the sea. There's a lift down to the promenade from where it is 10 minutes' walk to Puerto Rico beach or 15 minutes' walk to Amadores beach. ⓐ Avenida de la Cornisa, Puerto Rico ⓣ 928 128 505 ⓦ www.hotelgloriapalaceamadores.com

**La Hacienda del Buen Suceso £££** Aristocratic estate house in the middle of a banana plantation. Heated swimming pool. ⓐ Finca del Buen Suceso, Carretera de Arucas a Bañaderos, Arucas ⓣ 928 62 29 45 ⓦ www.haciendabuensuceso.com

**Santa Catalina £££** The island's luxury grand hotel which opened in 1890. Rooms either look out to sea or over the gardens. Bristling with facilities. ⓐ León y Castillo 227, Las Palmas ⓣ 928 23 40 40 ⓦ www.hotelsantacatalina.com

# Preparing to go

## GETTING THERE

The cheapest way to get to Gran Canaria is to book a package holiday with one of the leading tour operators specialising in Gran Canarian holidays. You should also check the travel supplements of the weekend newspapers, such as the *Sunday Telegraph* and the *Sunday Times*. They often carry adverts for inexpensive flights, as well as classified adverts for privately owned villas and apartments to rent in most popular holiday destinations.

If your travelling times are flexible, and if you can avoid the school holidays, you can also find some very cheap last-minute deals using the websites for the leading holiday companies.

### By air

The Canary Islands are a four-hour flight from the UK. The majority of visitors to the islands use charter companies, which operate from nearly all of the UK's regional airports. Only the Spanish national carrier, **Iberia Airlines**, offers scheduled flights to Gran Canaria, though this usually means changing in Madrid or Barcelona. ⓐ London Heathrow, ground floor, Terminal 2 ⓣ 0870 609 0500 ⓣ 0034 902 400 500 (24 hours – in Spain) ⓦ www.iberia.com

Search engines for cheap scheduled and charter flights include:
ⓦ www.lastminute.com
ⓦ www.flightline.co.uk
ⓦ www.flydeals.co.uk

The following companies offer cheap flights to Gran Canaria from the UK, departing from a wide variety of airports:
**easyJet** ⓦ www.easyjet.com
**First Choice** ⓦ www.firstchoice.co.uk/flights
**Globespan** ⓦ www.flyglobespan.co.uk
**Monarch** ⓦ www.flymonarch.com

**Ryanair** www.ryanair.com
**Thomas Cook** www.thomascook.com
**Thomsonfly** www.thomsonfly.com

Many people are aware that air travel emits $CO_2$, which contributes to climate change. You may be interested in the possibility of lessening the environmental impact of your flight through the charity **Climate Care**, which offsets your $CO_2$ by funding environmental projects around the world. Visit www.jpmorganclimatecare.com

Gran Canaria's airport is on the Bay of Gando, halfway down the east coast of the island, 25 km (15 miles) from Maspalomas and Playa del Inglés and 18 km (11 miles) from the capital, Las Palmas. It is on the north–south axis motorway, the GC1.

Bus route No 5 links the airport with Las Palmas and Maspalomas. Route No 60 also goes to Las Palmas and route No 66 also goes to Maspalomas. The bus stop is outside arrivals. There is a taxi rank adjacent to the bus stop. For taxi information: 928 154 777.

Car-hire companies have their desks on the ground floor between international arrivals and arrivals from the EU. They can be reached directly from baggage reclaim. Hire cars are collected from and returned to the ground floor of the car park.

Airport information 902 404 704 www.aena.es

## By ship

The only passenger and vehicle shipping line to operate a regular service between mainland Spain and the Canary Islands is the ferry company **Trasmediterranea** (trasmediterranea.es). Trasmediterranea's UK agent is **Southern Ferries** (30 Churton Street, London SW1V 2LP 0844 815 7785 www.southernferries.co.uk). Early bookings are necessary for school holidays and at carnival time (February). Tickets include all meals during the 48- to 72-hour voyage; pensioners get a 20 per cent discount.

## BEFORE YOU LEAVE

Holidays should be about fun and relaxation, so avoid last-minute panics and stress by making your preparations well in advance.

It is not necessary to have inoculations to travel in Europe, but you should make sure you and your family are up to date with the basics, such as tetanus. It is a good idea to pack a small first-aid kit to carry with you, containing plasters, antiseptic cream, travel sickness pills, insect repellent and/or bite relief cream, antihistamine tablets, upset stomach remedies and painkillers.

Sun lotion can be more expensive on Gran Canaria than in the UK, so it is worth taking a good selection, especially of the higher factor lotions if you have children with you, and don't forget after-sun cream as well. If you are taking prescription medicines, ensure that you take enough for the duration of your visit, and an extra copy of the information sheet in case of loss, but you may find it impossible to obtain the exact same medicines on Gran Canaria.

## ENTRY FORMALITIES

The most important documents you will need are your tickets and your passport. Check well in advance that your passport is up to date and has at least three months left to run (six months is even better). All children, including newborn babies, need their own passport. It takes at least three weeks to process a passport renewal. This can be longer in the run-up to the summer. Contact the **Identity & Passport Service** for the latest information (t 0300 222 0000 w www.direct.gov.uk/passports).

If you are a UK resident thinking of hiring a car while you are away, you will need to have your UK driving licence with you. If you want more than one driver for the car, the other drivers must have their licence too.

## MONEY

Spain entered the single currency on 1 January 2002. Euro (€) note denominations are 500, 200, 100, 50, 20, 10 and 5. Coins are 1 and 2 euros and 1, 2, 5, 10, 20 and 50 *céntimos*.

## TRAVEL INSURANCE

All UK residents are entitled to reduced cost or free medical treatment when temporarily visiting any country within the European Union (EU), including Spain. To obtain this treatment, you will need to obtain a European Health Insurance Card (EHIC) free of charge. For information and an application form, enquire at the post office or visit www.ehic.org.uk. You would only be covered for treatment provided under the state scheme at home. The government stresses that the European Health Insurance Card should not replace travel insurance and it is highly recommended that travellers cover themselves for unexpected costs, including medical emergency repatriation, and the loss of or damage to any belongings.

### Exchange

Traveller's cheques and Eurocheques can be used to pay bills or obtain money. Banks are open Monday to Friday 08.30–14.00 (some until 16.00); Saturday 09.00–13.00. Hotel receptions, travel agents and banks will exchange your cash, but *take note* that there are practically no exchange bureaux due to the euro being the European common currency now. Wherever you elect to change money, take your passport.

### Credit cards

These are accepted in all resorts.

## CLIMATE

Gran Canaria has so many tourists because the weather is almost guaranteed to be good. The average temperature ranges between 23 and 28°C (75 and 85°F). The island has three temperature belts. The north of the island, which includes Las Palmas southwards down to Vecindario, is the coolest band. The adjacent band runs from Vecindario south to Playa del Inglés, and the band next to this runs from Playa del Inglés to the southern tip of the island, which includes Puerto Rico and

Mogán. Each one of these bands has a temperature variation of 2°C (3–4°F) from the adjacent one, with the hottest band being in the south. The weather can be quite a bit cooler in the mountains, especially between the months of November to the end of May, so always take a light jacket or cardigan with you if you go during these months.

Because the island is much closer to the equator than many other holiday areas, fair-skinned people will burn very quickly, even on a cloudy day. Always take precautions against the sun.

## BAGGAGE ALLOWANCES

Baggage allowances vary according to the airline, destination and the class of travel. Check with your airline before departure. In general, 15–20 kg (33–44 lb) per person is the norm for luggage that is carried in the hold (it usually tells you what the weight limit is on your ticket). You are also allowed one item of cabin baggage usually weighing no more than 5 kg (11 lb), though some airlines allow 10 kg (22 lb), and measuring 46 by 30 by 23 cm (18 by 12 by 9 in). In addition, you can carry your duty-free purchases, umbrella, handbag, coat, camera, etc, as hand baggage. Large items – surfboards, golf clubs, collapsible wheelchairs and pushchairs – are usually charged as extras and it is a good idea to let the airline know in advance that you want to bring these.

# During your stay

## AIRPORTS

The airport on Gran Canaria caters very well for tourists, with a range of sandwich bars and a restaurant. There is always a cafeteria open for drinks and snacks for those who have to leave during the night. There is also a children's play area where the little ones can while away the waiting time for the flight. There is a wide selection of shops for last-minute purchases, gifts and for local crafts, ceramics and plants. These shops are open from 08.00 to 21.00. The duty-free shop opens at the same time, but closes later, depending on whether there is anyone in the shop. When buying things from the airport, remember that most things are cheaper in the resort areas.

## COMMUNICATIONS

### Telephones

The island has an abundance of public telephones. Some take cards and some coins. Most phone booths on Gran Canaria have multilingual instructions. You can buy international phonecards in most shops. To use a public phone, first lift the receiver and wait for a tone and for a display asking you to introduce money or a card. Insert coins or a card, and then push the numbered buttons to dial. When you have finished, you may get some change or the card will be returned with unused credits.

You can also call from your hotel room, but be aware of the cost involved. The cheapest time to call home is after 20.00, and all day Saturday and Sunday and public holidays.

### Post

The postal service in Spain is called *correos*. You'll find large post offices in the major towns, which generally open 08.30–20.30 Monday to Friday and 09.30–13.00 on Saturday. Smaller post offices in outlying towns and villages may only be open in the morning until 14.30. Post boxes on Gran Canaria are easy to spot since they are bright yellow.

**TELEPHONING GRAN CANARIA**

To call Gran Canaria from the UK, dial 00 34 for Spain, followed by 928 (the Gran Canaria area code), followed by the six-digit number.

**TELEPHONING ABROAD**

The dialling code for international access is 00. Follow this by the country code (USA and Canada 1, UK 44, France 33, Italy 39, Australia 61) and then the area code, usually losing the initial 0.

### Internet

All the major resorts and towns have Internet cafés. Some hotels offer broadband Internet access in the rooms. There are wireless Internet hotspots covering parts of resorts such as Maspalomas, Playa del Inglés and Puerto Rico.

## CUSTOMS

Tourism has only come to the Canaries within the last 20 to 30 years, so there are not many customs the locals expect tourists to uphold. However, it is worth trying to speak some Spanish, even if you can only manage a very little. There are no restrictions on entering the churches, but respectful behaviour is expected (not making a lot of noise, no smoking, eating or drinking).

Topless sunbathing is common on most beaches. There are 40 designated naturist beaches around the island where some people (but not all) strip off completely: ask at any tourist information office to find the nearest one. **Magnolias Natura** (W www.canariasnatura.com) is a naturist bungalow complex next to Maspalomas golf course (see page 106).

## DRESS CODES

There is no particular dress code for Gran Canaria, but it is respectful not to wear your skimpy shorts and tops in the larger towns and to keep these for the beach resorts.

## ELECTRICITY

You will need an adaptor plug for electrical appliances, which can be bought from any major retail outlet in the UK or from most of the tourist shops on the island. The voltage is 220, slightly less than in the UK, but it won't affect the appliance. If you are not careful when removing a plug in your hotel room, the whole electrical socket could come out as well! It is not advisable to use electrical appliances from the USA on this voltage system. If you are buying electrical appliances to take home, always check that they will work in your country before you buy.

## EMERGENCIES

### UK Consulate

The British Consulate in Las Palmas has British staff as well as some Spanish staff who speak excellent English. You can sometimes catch them (by telephone) 30 minutes before and after opening and closing hours. ⓣ 928 26 25 08/26 58 (it may be engaged for some time) 🕒 08.00–13.30 Mon–Fri except national holidays, closed Sat & Sun

### EMERGENCY NUMBERS

For an ambulance or help in an emergency, call:

**Red Cross emergency service** ⓣ 222 222

**Paramedics' freephone** ⓣ 061 or 112

**Police** ⓣ 091

## GAY TRAVELLERS

Gran Canaria styles itself as one of Europe's principal gay destinations and it has an extensive choice of gay-friendly or exclusively gay accommodation, as well as gay bars and clubs and nominally gay beaches. Maspalomas and Playa del Inglés are the centre of the action, with Las Palmas close behind. The Yumbo Centrum in Playa del Inglés is said to be the largest group of gay bars, restaurants and nightspots in

Europe. Maspalomas has a famous gay beach backed by sand dunes which provide intimate spaces for sunbathing.

## GETTING AROUND

### Driving

**Car hire** In Spain and its islands this has become increasingly competitive. Before you go, check out the various price-comparison websites for the best deals. Once on the island, shop around for local companies – even in high season you'll find they are in serious competition with each other. Some companies will take a deposit to cover any insurance excess if the car is damaged. Some will also charge you for a tank of petrol, while others will not charge you for fuel, but will expect the car to be returned full. When collecting the car, you'll need to present both parts of your driving licence and a valid credit card, usually the one you booked your car with.

When driving a hired car in Spain, all documents (insurance information, rental information and your driving licence) must be carried in the car. If stopped, the police require the originals, not photocopies, nor can you present your documents at a police station at a later date.

**Rules of the road** Driving in Spain is not the same as in the UK. It is not just a matter of driving on the right. Watch the road signals carefully, give way to any traffic on roundabouts, don't be pushed into doing something because someone has his finger stuck on the hooter behind you, and be careful on some crossroads where, in order to turn left, you have first of all to turn right and then cross the road you were originally driving on.

The only fast roads on the island are the *autopistas* (motorways), the GC1, GC2 and the GC3. The main route, the GC1, runs from Las Palmas down to the southern tip of the island at Puerto Rico. This one serves the airport. The GC2 runs out of Las Palmas along the northern coast as far as Guía at present. The GC3 intersects at Jinamer on the GC1 and circumnavigates Las Palmas/Tamaraceite, heading north to join the GC2 to Guía. There is also a short section of GC3 motorway which goes off to Tafira Alta, from where you continue on the usual road to Santa Brígida/San Mateo. The speed limit on these roads is 120 km/h (75 mph), unless otherwise advised. On *carreteras* (dual carriageways) the limit is 80 km/h (50 mph), and in built-up areas it is 40 km/h (25 mph) or 30 km/h (19 mph). Motorists must carry their driving licence, passport, insurance and car-hire documents at all times. Failure to do so will result in an on-the-spot fine if stopped at one of the frequent road checks.

**Road conditions** The road surfaces are generally good, but many mountain roads are particularly narrow and winding. Nervous drivers might feel uncomfortable at first on some mountain roads, but safety barriers are well employed. Care and patience are all that are needed for safe driving.

**Road markings** These are generally clear but some of the traffic systems, especially those around motorway junctions, can be confusing when first encountered. Be aware that traffic priorities in these complex traffic systems do not always conform to European practice and you might suddenly find a stop sign on a main route.

**Breaking down** If your car does break down, in compliance with European Union laws, you must place red warning triangles 100 m (110 yds) in front of and behind your vehicle. The police *will* fine you if you don't. Therefore, it is always wise to check that you have them in your car. Then, all you need to do is to phone the 24-hour service number written on your insurance document or on the card which the car-hire firm gave you, asking the representative if there are English-speaking people on the switchboard.

## Public transport

**Buses** There is an extremely good bus service, called Global, which runs buses all over the island. It has a 24-hour service going to and from Playa del Inglés to Las Palmas. Up to 23.00, there are several buses per hour and they pass through Playa del Inglés itself. After 23.00, there is one bus per hour throughout the night until 06.00, but this bus goes along the bypass outside of Playa del Inglés. The last bus from Mogán through Puerto Rico and on to Las Palmas leaves at 19.30; the first bus in the morning leaves at 08.10. From Las Palmas to Mogán, the first bus in the morning leaves at 05.40 and the last one leaves at 19.40. If you want any other information about other bus routes and times, there are timetables on most bus stops, or you can go to the Global office in the Yumbo Centrum.

Season tickets (*bonos*) are available at the Yumbo Centrum at all shops displaying a Global sign and also at the bus station in Las Palmas. If you think that you are going to make quite a few journeys on the same route, it is well worth looking into, because the saving is about 30 per cent. Two or more people can use the same *bono*.

The Canarian word for bus is *guagua*, pronounced 'wah-wah'.

**Bus information:** ⓦ www.globalsu.net ⓣ 928 25 26 30

**Taxis** These are very reasonable and if there are more than two in your party, it could work out cheaper than going by bus. The best thing to do is to ask a taxi driver how much the fare would be to where you are going and then compare it with the bus fares.

**Ferries** A complex network of inter-island ferries and hydrofoils links the seven main islands of the Canaries, and schedules change very regularly, so you need to check times locally. To reach La Palma, La Gomera, El Hierro and Fuerteventura, it is necessary to take the inter-island ferries. Most of the inter-island services are operated by Trasmediterranea (all passenger enquiries, see 'By ship', page 109) or the **Fred Olsen Line** (ⓐ Edificio Fred Olsen, Polígono Industrial Añaza, Santa Cruz de Tenerife ⓣ 928 49 50 46/902 10 01 07 ⓕ 928 49 50 31 for timetable details and booking ⓦ www.fredolsen.es). The local airline **Binter Canarias** provides regular flights between the islands (ⓐ Aeropuerto de Gran Canaria, Parcela 9 del ZIMA, Apartado 50, 35230 Gran Canaria ⓣ 928 57 96 01/902 39 13 92 booking number ⓦ www.bintercanarias.es).

## HEALTH, SAFETY & CRIME

**Beaches** In summer, many beaches have lifeguards and a flag safety system. Other beaches may be safe for swimming but there are unlikely to be lifeguards or life-saving amenities available. Bear in mind that the

**BEACH SAFETY**

Most beaches where the public bathe in numbers operate a flag system to indicate the sea conditions.

- Red (or black): dangerous – no swimming
- Yellow: good swimmers only – apply caution
- Green (or white): safe bathing conditions for all

strong winds in the hotter months can quickly change a safe beach into a not-so-safe one, and some can have strong currents the further out that you go. If in doubt, ask your local representative or at your hotel.

**Children** Be careful not to go to places like Palmitos Park, Sioux City or any of the water parks if it is a really scorching hot day. There are many things to do in the evening, when the heat of the sun has gone. There is the mini-train, and most of the big shopping/restaurant complexes, like the Cita and along the Avenida de Tirajana in Playa del Inglés, have a mini-golf and skittles area.

If you go to any of the animal or plant parks, remember to take plenty of drinking water with you, as you will probably be walking around for a good few hours. Always make sure that you wear some sort of protective covering on your heads. All of the water parks forbid the wearing of T-shirts when on any of the apparatus, which means that children are advised to wear their T-shirts until the last moment when queuing for a slide to avoid excessive exposure to the sun.

**Emergency dental and medical care** Private clinics around the resorts are very well equipped for any medical or dental emergency, but if they cannot provide the necessary treatment, arrangements will be made to transfer you to a larger clinic or one of the hospitals. If you do not have private insurance but have a European Health Insurance Card, you must go directly to one of the National Health clinics or hospitals, remembering to take your passport with you. The standard of treatment and care is very high.

**Private clinics** Several private clinics with English-speaking staff offer 24-hour emergency medical assistance, including an ambulance service. For these clinics, take your flight tickets and travel insurance policy.
**Medical Salud Las Palmeras** ⓐ Avenida de Tenerife, Playa del Inglés ⓣ 928 76 29 92/93. They have a second location at ⓐ Fase 2, Centro Cívico Comercial Puerto Rico ⓣ 928 56 12 87
**Clínica Roca** A private hospital. ⓐ Buganvilla 1, San Agustín ⓣ 928 76 92 08/90 04 ⓦ www.clinicaroca.com

**Health hazards** Even with a breeze blowing, the sun is very strong and you should not stay out in it too long, especially between 12.00 and 16.00. Appropriate sun creams/blocks and sun apparel should be worn at all times. If you go walking anywhere in the countryside, even for a short stroll to have a break from the beach, go prepared. Always carry water and wear a sunhat, and make sure that someone knows where you've gone and when you expect to be back.

**Medicines** If you have to take regular medication, always ensure that you bring enough to last for the duration of your stay. If you lose your medication and you have brought the leaflet or a repeat prescription, then a doctor/chemist may provide you with the same or equivalent drug.

**Condoms** These can be bought from any chemist, supermarket, other retail outlets and most men's toilets.

**Water** While the local tap water on Gran Canaria will not harm you, it is not really advisable to drink it. The exception is in the town of Firgas (see page 24), which is famous for its spring water that is bottled and sold all over the island. You can buy it and other brands of bottled water from any of the supermarkets. For any other parts of the island, bottled water is recommended for making tea and coffee, and for cleaning your teeth.

**Crime** As in any other tourist resort, valuables left lying unattended or in cars may be stolen. Men should not put their wallets in their back trouser pocket because there are pickpockets around. Women should avoid carrying a handbag with a strap over the shoulder because it could easily be snatched by someone running past or driving past on a motorbike. There is little incidence of violent crime on Gran Canaria.

**Lost property** Depending on where you lose it, you should first ask if it has been handed in. If it is something valuable or important, then you have to go to the police station (on the bypass, opposite the Hotel Buenaventura) to file a complaint (*una denuncia*). Before going there, however, contact the tour representative to ask them if they can provide you with an interpreter if you can't speak Spanish, or take someone who does, because the police will not deal with you if you do not speak the language. Remember, if your credit cards are stolen, you must contact the companies' main offices immediately to inform them and they will cancel them so that you lose as little money as possible.

**Making a complaint** If you have any complaint about the hotel/ complex, then it is always advisable to try and rectify it first with the staff and management. However, if nothing is done to alleviate the problem, then you should see your tour representative.

**Police** The local police (in blue uniforms) do not make their appearance too overpowering, but they do walk along the prom and drive around in efforts to prevent crime from happening. On the roads, you will see the traffic police, the Guardia Civil. They wear green uniforms and ride motorbikes or drive cars, and they take their job very seriously. The National Police wear navy trousers and jackets with white shirts. They deal with serious crime, drug offences, etc.

## MEDIA

**Cinemas** Most films shown are dubbed into Spanish but some English-language films are shown, particularly in areas with high

concentrations of foreign residents. Some mainstream films also show films with subtitles. These are indicated as 'V.O.' on posters (for *versión original*)

**Newspapers** UK daily and Sunday papers are widely available in supermarkets and on newsstands (*kioscos*) in the resorts and larger towns. Some editions can be bought on the day but others will be a day old. The free English-language newspaper *Round Town News* (ⓦ www.roundtownnews.co.uk) can be picked up in many bars, restaurants and shops and has useful news about events and adverts for local services. Another useful publication is *Island Connections* (ⓦ www.islandconnections.eu), which is distributed on all the islands.

**Radio** For UK news on the hour, sports and lottery results, as well as 24-hour music, tune in to QFM on FM98.

**Television** In any of the hotels or complexes that have televisions installed, you can usually get one or two English channels, normally Sky News and a Sky film channel. Football fans can watch league matches and all major tournament finals in most of the English bars.

## OPENING HOURS

**Banks** are open Monday to Friday from 08.30 to 14.00, some on Saturday from 08.30 to 13.00.

If they are large, **churches** are open during the day until about 20.00, but the smaller ones may open only during service hours and/or on Sundays.

**Museums** are generally open daily from 09.00 to 19.30, Monday to Saturday, but it is advisable to telephone and check.

**Pharmacies** have the same opening times as shops but do not open on Sunday. However, there is always a duty pharmacy (*Farmacia de Guardia*) open 24 hours a day somewhere in the area. There is a list of these on each pharmacy door. In a resort the size of Playa del Inglés, there are probably two or three that are open 24 hours. They rotate the duty days.

**Restaurants** usually open daily and on public holidays as well.

Most **shops** in the resorts open from 09.00 to 13.00 and from 16.00 to 20.00, Monday to Saturday, and some supermarkets open on a Sunday from 09.00 to 13.00.

## RELIGION

There are religious buildings of all the major faiths on the island. In Playa del Inglés, there is the Ecumenical church in the main square, which holds services for Protestants and Roman Catholics. There is a Jehovah's Witness temple in San Fernando, Vecindario and Las Palmas. Baptist and Nonconformist churches can be found in Las Palmas, as can the mosque.

## TIME DIFFERENCES

The time is always the same as that of the UK. The clocks change in spring and autumn on the same day at the same time.

## TIPPING

It isn't obligatory to tip, and, if you do, it should be because the meal and the service warrant it. The usual amount to leave is 5 to 10 per cent of the total bill.

## TOILETS

There are any number of public toilets in the resorts, in cafés, restaurants, shops and the airport. They are very clean and some have an attendant who will expect a small gratuity.

## TOURIST INFORMATION

Gran Canaria has tourist information offices in just about every town, where visitors can get information on everything they may need to know. They all have the same opening hours: 09.00–14.00, 15.00–20.00 Mon–Fri, 09.00–13.00 Sat, closed Sun (summer); 09.00–22.00 Mon–Fri, 09.00–13.00 Sat, closed Sun (winter)

**Airport** ⓐ Arrivals hall ⓣ 928 57 41 17

**La Aldea de San Nicolás** ⓐ Calle Doctor Fleming 57, San Nicolás ⓣ 928 890 378 ⓦ www.la-aldea.com

**Gáldar** ⓐ Plaza de Santiago 1 ⓣ 928 895 855 ⓦ www.galdar.es

**Las Palmas** ⓐ Parque Santa Catalina ⓣ 928 26 46 23 ⓦ www.laspalmasgc.es

**Playa del Inglés** This is the main tourist office and is excellent, providing free maps and lots of local information, including printed bus timetables. ⓐ Avenida de España (adjacent to the Yumbo Centrum) ⓣ 928 77 15 50 ⓦ www.grancanaria.com

**Puerto Rico** ⓐ Avenida de Mogán ⓣ 928 56 00 29 ⓦ www.turismo.mogan.es

**Tejeda** ⓐ Leocadio Cabrera ⓣ 928 66 61 89 ⓦ www.tejeda.es

All offices should have at least one English-speaking member of staff and be able to advise you on accommodation, public transport, walks in the area and local events.

Also useful for planning a trip to Gran Canaria is the main Spanish tourism website: ⓦ www.spaininfo.com

## TRAVELLERS WITH DISABILITIES

In all the newer shopping centres, hotels and complexes, there are facilities such as ramps, wider passageways, special lifts and toilets for visitors with disabilities. In the older areas, it is a little more hit-and-miss, but on the whole you shouldn't have any problems. Most facilities are in the process of being updated according to EU specifications, and all pavements now have ramps for wheelchairs.

## M



## N



## O



## P



## Q



## R



## S



## T



## V



## W



## Z

**ACKNOWLEDGEMENTS**

We would like to thank all the photographers, picture libraries and organisations for the loan of the photographs reproduced in this book, to whom copyright in the photograph belongs:
Dreamstime Juriah Mosin (page 72), E Ayuso (pages 25, 80), R Clarke (page 105); Joe Cawley (pages 18, 60, 62); Thomas Cook (pages 5, 10–11, 13, 31, 39, 40, 44, 47, 51, 65, 67, 83, 85, 86, 88, 92, 96, 98); Wikimedia Commons M Perdomo (page 56), Thomas Tolkien (page 69); World Pictures/Photoshot (pages 58, 71, 75, 76, 94)

Project editor: Rosalind Munro
Layout: Donna Pedley
Proofreaders: Cath Senker & Kelly Walker
Indexer: Marie Lorimer

**Send your thoughts to**
**books@thomascook.com**

- **Found a beach bar, peaceful stretch of sand or must-see sight that we don't feature?**
- **Like to tip us off about any information that needs a little updating?**
- **Want to tell us what you love about this handy, little guidebook and, more importantly, how we can make it even handier?**

Then here's your chance to tell all! Send us ideas, discoveries and recommendations today and then look out for your valuable input in the next edition of this title.

Email to the above address or write to:
pocket guides Series Editor, Thomas Cook Publishing, PO Box 227, Unit 9, Coningsby Road, Peterborough PE3 8SB, UK.

# Useful phrases

| English | Spanish | *Approx pronunciation* |
|---|---|---|
| **BASICS** | | |
| **Yes** | Sí | *Si* |
| **No** | No | *Noh* |
| **Please** | Por favor | *Por fabor* |
| **Thank you** | Gracias | *Grathias* |
| **Hello** | Hola | *Ola* |
| **Goodbye** | Adiós | *Adios* |
| **Excuse me** | Disculpe | *Diskoolpeh* |
| **Sorry** | Perdón | *Pairdohn* |
| **That's okay** | De acuerdo | *Dey acwerdo* |
| **I don't speak Spanish** | No hablo español | *Noh ablo espanyol* |
| **Do you speak English?** | ¿Habla Usted inglés? | *¿Abla oosteth eengless?* |
| **Good morning** | Buenos días | *Bwenos dee-as* |
| **Good afternoon** | Buenas tardes | *Bwenas tarrdess* |
| **Good evening** | Buenas noches | *Bwenas notchess* |
| **Goodnight** | Buenas noches | *Bwenas notchess* |
| **My name is ...** | Me llamo ... | *Meh yiamo ...* |
| **NUMBERS** | | |
| **One** | Uno | *Oono* |
| **Two** | Dos | *Dos* |
| **Three** | Tres | *Tres* |
| **Four** | Cuatro | *Cwatro* |
| **Five** | Cinco | *Thinco* |
| **Six** | Seis | *Seys* |
| **Seven** | Siete | *Seeyetey* |
| **Eight** | Ocho | *Ocho* |
| **Nine** | Nueve | *Nwebeyh* |
| **Ten** | Diez | *Deeyeth* |
| **Twenty** | Veinte | *Beintey* |
| **Fifty** | Cincuenta | *Thincwenta* |
| **One hundred** | Cien | *Thien* |
| **SIGNS & NOTICES** | | |
| **Airport** | Aeropuerto | *Aehropwerto* |
| **Railway station** | Estación de trenes | *Estathion de trenes* |
| **Platform** | Vía | *Via* |
| **Smoking/ non-smoking** | Fumadores/ No fumadores | *Foomadoores/ No foomadores* |
| **Toilets** | Servicios | *Serbitheeos* |
| **Ladies/Gentlemen** | Señoras/Caballeros | *Senyoras/Kabayeros* |